SUPPLY CHAIN SECURITY

A Comprehensive Approach

SUPPLY CHAIN SECURITY

A Comprehensive Approach

DR. ARTHUR G. ARWAY

CRC Press
Taylor & Francis Group
Boca Raton   London   New York

CRC Press is an imprint of the
Taylor & Francis Group, an **informa** business

CRC Press
Taylor & Francis Group
6000 Broken Sound Parkway NW, Suite 300
Boca Raton, FL 33487-2742

© 2013 by Taylor & Francis Group, LLC
CRC Press is an imprint of Taylor & Francis Group, an Informa business

No claim to original U.S. Government works

Printed on Acid-free paper
Version Date: 20130114

International Standard Book Number-13: 978-1-4665-1187-3 (Hardback)

Visit the Taylor & Francis Web site at
http://www.taylorandfrancis.com

and the CRC Press Web site at
http://www.crcpress.com

To Bob Ghan, Nick DiRaimondo, Enrique Gonzalez, and Bryan Hrapchak—the best supply chain security practitioners in the business who taught me well. And to my wife and honey, Dr. Rosemary Arway, who encouraged me to move forward with this book. Thank you.

Contents

List of Figures

About the Author

Dr. Arthur G. Arway is a recognized leader in domestic and international logistics, trade, and transportation security. He provides significant experiential horsepower to both the managerial and practical sides of supply chain security.

He brings to the table 27-plus years of supply chain cargo security, law enforcement, investigative, human resource, and corporate security experience.

He has been responsible for domestic and international protection programs in the Americas and other global regions for client material, operations, transportation, freight, cargo, parcel and lightweight industry, government supply chain program compliance, TSA cargo security programs, client security interface, sales and marketing support and risk mitigation for corporate legal, risk management, and HR business units.

His supply chain security career has placed him, among other noteworthy positions, deeply integrated into a major international logistic organization. He is an advisor to senior management as well as governmental security agencies.

Dr. Arway has contributed to the body of work on supply chain and logistics security and has been cited in trade publications such as *Journal of Commerce*, *CargoVision*, and the on-line logistics magazine, *DCVelocity*.

As a Certified Protection Professional (CPP) with ASIS International, he has presented at numerous industry meetings and exhibitions. He has been honored by ASIS International with the Golden Writers Award for his work on workplace violence.

He is also a contributing chapter author in *Violence at Work: Causes, Patterns and Prevention* (Willan Press).

Beginning his career with law enforcement, Dr. Arway successfully rose through the ranks, while expanding his education, leading to receiving his Doctorate of Business degree from the University of Sarasota, FL.

Introduction

The world of supply chain security operates in a harsh environment. It is not for the faint of heart. It is not a hobby. It is not a part-time job. The environment is intense, relentless, and indifferent to sensibility and civilized culture. It preys upon the weak, the unaware, the complacent, and the ill-prepared. Any gap, anywhere, at any time, can be detected and exploited.

Protecting the supply chain provides a variety of qualities. Goods, products, and materials need to be delivered intact to be useful to industry and consumers. These materials generate revenue for companies and industries that, in turn, provide a livelihood for people and their families. Compromised material is useless and a drain on manufacturing. Quality can suffer; products can be delayed or made to be inferior. Supply chain security also can help to protect citizens and civilization from the evils of criminality and terrorism. In other words, security, and specifically supply chain security, is serious business. It provides a worthwhile service to industries, consumers, corporations, and governments.

What we hope to accomplish in this text is to elucidate how all this operates. We will look at its components and mechanisms and see how they interact with each other and with the supply chain to effectively protect the flow of goods in and around the globe. There are a number of books on security that detail security services, devices, products, technology, applications, etc. While we do touch on some of these topics, it is not our attempt to re-explain and educate the reader on these practicalities and specific applications. Rather, we hope to show the importance of security within the supply chain, how it not only protects the materials, but how it may enhance the fiscal well-being of the owners or handlers of the goods and services operating and using the supply chain. I will also add here that this book is not intended to be a primer on supply chain security. You will not see specific details on the design and use of security technology devices and programs. I do use some of these to illustrate how they can enhance the security of clients' or customers' supply chains. There are numerous articles, publications, and providers who can give you all the applications you may need. The discussions contained herein target the managers (or those aspiring to be) in the field of supply chain security.

We hope to weave a tapestry of integrated threads and methodologies together here, which in turn creates and develops an overarching philosophy for securing the supply chain. You will see how security measures have rippling effects all along the chain and how collateral damage can be contained and externalities produced.

We are attempting to instill a culture of security in and around the supply chain. Simply following our suggestions and guidelines is mechanical. However, knowing why there should be security at a given point or maneuver and being aware of the impact of the absence or presence of security—and knowing the difference—is a product of culture.

There are other dimensions at work to support your security program. This sounds trite, but foremost is leadership by example. You have to beat the drum for security. If you don't, few others will pay attention. It is a constant sell. Businesses and companies are focused on the P&L (profit and loss) sheet. Your job is to show them that security will positively affect the bottom line. Companies pay attention to programs that either make them money or save them money. It is rare that security will be a revenue- or income-based cost center. So, the value of supply chain security is that your program can attract business, ergo revenue, or save money through reduced losses, claims, and insurance premiums and better customer retention. Don't wait for upper management to come to you; that is reactive. Go to them with a business case and be proactive.

Also don't be afraid to use security events or failures to learn from for future situations. Take a failure, loss, or other security incident and turn it into "an unfortunate security marketing opportunity." Take the causes of the event and sell your security program as both a short- and long-term fix. Do this always, even if it is not always accepted. This will show the viability of your program as well as your dedication to the program and leadership within the organization.

I have included several case studies for your review. These will help you understand how supply chain security is different from traditional corporate security. It will also show you that supply chain security is multifaceted with many moving parts that depend upon several, or many, people and processes to be truly effective.

Each of these case studies was chosen to show different applications of supply chain security. They are all true events and situations. Of course, I have completely changed all identifying references to people, companies, and locations for their protection and to preserve their anonymity. However, the circumstances I provide are actual events, not only for these situations, but also for other current and future situations, customers, locations, etc., that could be at risk. These were learning opportunities and perfect examples of that *unfortunate security marketing opportunity*.

PART I

WHAT IS SUPPLY CHAIN SECURITY?

1

WHAT IS A SUPPLY CHAIN?

For the purposes of this publication, we will need to define what it is that commonly comprises a supply chain and how all the links are interconnected through the lens of security. There are other versions for other applications, which can be similar. As we move ahead in our discussion of supply chain security, we need a benchmark, or at least a reference point, on what we mean by *supply chain*, including its components and relationships.

A supply chain is just that. It is a chain of interconnected links that facilitates the movement of *supplies*, or in other words, cargo, goods, material, products, etc. This chain can be very short with only a few links and handoffs, or it can be lengthy, far reaching, and complex, with dozens of links and handoffs. In the field of supply chain security, it is very important to have an understanding of the elements of a supply chain, both on academic and on practical levels. This is important, as in any serious endeavor. This way we can effectively understand what it is that is expected and what is the correct function or application of the link. We can then recognize what might be misaligned or askew and what can be done to correct the issue and protect it moving forward.

We will start at the beginning, otherwise termed as the *origin*. Then we will progress through the traditional links of the supply chain and then talk about how to best secure those portions. There is no one overall security panacea for the protection of the supply chain. To be truly effective, each link and handoff has to be examined, understood, and protected.

1.1 Origin

As mentioned previously, we need to understand what it is that we are looking at and have a common agreement as to its use, function, and how we can apply a security program. Be careful to know how participants using that portion of the chain define the term. Even the term *origin* has to be examined, and an agreement needs to be in place for you to fully appreciate what it is that will be required and what risks, even liability, exist within that link.

Origin generally means where the material is first introduced into the supply chain. Many security risks to material exist prior to being introduced into the chain. If you are responsible for the security of this portion, you will need to be sure if you are also responsible for the material prior to being added to your link. Very often, customers will indicate what they require or what you will need to provide by way of security for the material starting at origin. You must clearly research what the customer/client expects and how you might be held liable. We will talk more about this later, but you always should keep in mind the potential liability from both a security-program and a risk-management angle. A failure, theft, pilferage, or penetration will focus on a security breach, and someone will be liable for the monetary cost of the loss.

1.2 Manufacturing/Suppliers

Many clients have or own their own plants, mills, etc., and ship to their own places of manufacture or assembly, or ship to their customers who utilize that material. Others procure material from other suppliers and then manufacture or distribute them for their own use or to others. You might be called upon to secure from that initial point of acquirement, or possibly from the time when they are ready to send out manufactured goods to distribution centers (DCs) or customers (see Figure 1.1).

In any event, this is usually the beginning of the supply chain. Goods are brought together, packaged for shipment, and then sent on their way through the chain to an expected end point. In some cases, logistics providers are hired to consolidate the materials from manufacturers/suppliers and to develop and apply appropriate packing for transportation and delivery.

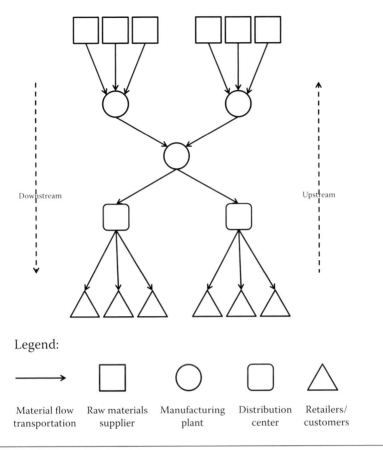

Figure 1.1   Basic supply chain matrix.

1.3 Handoffs

This is usually the point of transfer to a service provider in the movement of the material. These transfers are known as handoffs. The client hands off or passes the material from their own possession, or from the possession of one of their agents or suppliers, to another for handling and possible transportation. Go back and look at Figure 1.1. A handoff occurs each time one function touches another.

This handoff is important, as there is also an exchange of paperwork that in most cases describes the material, manifests, packing slips, invoices, the current packing configurations, dimensions (DIMs—weight/height/length/width), condition of the material, and in some cases, values and government tax and tariff documents.

On the receiving end of the handoff is the custody portion of the transaction. Whoever is accepting this material is now in a custodial position until they complete their portion and hand it off to another.

1.4 Initial Service Provider

Along the chain there can be many providers of a variety of modes, but initially the first providers are generally ground transports from the site of manufacture to another destination for use by the client. These ground transportation providers can move from distances of short city streets to full cross-country long hauls.

1.5 Service Providers

As described previously, the first provider is usually ground transportation, or trucking. In some bulk instances, material is handed off directly to a rail provider using a rail siding or spur on the client's property.

1.6 Trucking

Trucking operations are used in all corners of the globe, and all have similar uses and issues as well as similar security concerns. For the purposes of this discussion about understanding the security of the supply chain, we will look at two major methods of trucking: line haul and hub and spoke (see Figure 1.2).

Hub and spoke is just as it sounds. Trucks bring material into a center point or hub, and then transfer cargo to other trucks going to other destinations, like spokes in a wheel. The hub and spoke is a distribution type of network. Trucks that pick up material at a variety of locations in their assigned territories then bring these materials to a central facility that services a number of spokes or territories. These trucks are considered LTLs (less than full trailer loads). This means that the trailer is not loaded with the intent to deliver to only one destination. Some trucking facilities might fill a trailer at only one stop, but the intent is to bring all that material to a hub where it can be broken down, or redistributed, to other destinations. This creates efficiency for the trucking firms instead of having a truck drive to multiple destinations that can be at long distances or using

Figure 1.2 Truck hauler.

complicated and time- and resource-consuming routes. Hub-and-spoke operations are points of handoff and pose a concern for the security professional. The material is off-loaded, separated by destination, and moved to other parts of the operation, to be placed with other materials from other sources and then set upon other trucks for other destinations.

Once the material is sorted, it is loaded onto a truck destined for another region where the client wishes the material to be delivered or passed to another mode, or type, of provider. In some instances, the spoke destination is another hub in a far-reaching location. This usually occurs when that hub services a nearby region or another service provider. At the same time, any accompanying paperwork must follow the material to comply with the client's business and government transportation regulations. Each pickup, spoke, hub, handoff, and destination is a security threat and needs to be examined.

Line-haul (sometimes referred to as long haul) moves are different in that they take a load usually of one type of material or material from one client in an FTL (full trailer load) capacity to a single destination in another region, state, or even another country. This destination could be a distribution center or a direct delivery to a customer or a provider.

The handoffs for a line haul are limited. Usually it is done once at the origin location, then once at the destination. When finished, that particular trucking provider is released. There is no re-sorting, handling, etc., of concern to the provider.

1.7 Ocean Shipping

Providers who transport material via the high seas are the ocean providers. Container ships of many types embark and disembark material of all types using shipping lanes that crisscross the oceans between the continents. The speed of the ships can be, on average, 25 knots, or approximately 28 mph, over water. Depending upon the size, load, capacity, and weather, a shipment, moving from a North Atlantic port to a port on the west shore of Latin America could take anywhere from seven to eleven weeks (see Figure 1.3).

The relationship of an ocean provider to the supply chain is as a service provider who has been handed material, via either trucking or rail, and then moves this material to another port to be handed off to another provider for ground transport via either rail or trucking. Many ports around the world have railheads on their properties that have ocean box containers already loaded onto their rail cars, which

Figure 1.3 Ocean shipping.

are off-loaded directly to ocean port staging areas. The converse is also true.

There are number of handoff procedures that take place for ocean shipping. They generally involve receiving a loaded ocean container that is then loaded and off-loaded as requested. Port authorities, both local and national, have regulations that impact ocean shipping. Some of these address security, but they do not cover everything that can place material at a security vulnerability or risk.

Many ocean ports have their own internal form of trucking. These allow for the movement of the ocean containers as needed for staging, inspection, etc. They also move containers in and out of off-port property-holding yards to help in reducing congestion within the confines of the shipyards. This is another security concern that we will look at later.

Once the loaded ship reaches the desired destination port for the client material, the box is handed off to another trucking provider. This provider could take it to an end point or another handoff to a distribution center. This could be done by line haul or moving within another hub-and-spoke network.

Ocean carriers are often chosen to transport material because they can haul great loads of raw material like oil or grain from source continents to consumer or manufacturing continents. Also, used as container shipping, goods can be shipped for far less cost than shipping by air. The ocean cargo delivery times are, of course, more spread out, but when these time frames are calculated, they fit easily into client delivery and production schedules.

1.8 Airlines

Airlines, as a supply chain link, handle great volumes of cargo and material. Of course, they are also passenger carriers (which you often see coded as PAX). There is an entire segment of this industry, known as all-cargo or freighters, that is dedicated only to cargo and material (see Figure 1.4).

Airlines are utilized for any number of reasons. The most common are speed and material condition. The first, speed, is important due to the ability to deliver material quickly over large distances. Client production or contractual obligations may dictate the material needs

Figure 1.4 Airline shipping.

to arrive on a specified point in time when the material origin is far removed from the destination. The other is the criticality of maintaining the material's condition, as in the case of pharmaceuticals, which can be sensitive to variations in time and temperature. The faster they are packaged and delivered, the less risk to their certifications or spoilage factors. It stands to reason that a load of fresh flowers needs to be received by the customer as fast as possible. Time in transit is critical for some materials coming from producers in Latin America that are being distributed to many global points.

The different types of air transportation—PAX or all cargo—handle cargo in a similar fashion. However, when developing a security plan for client cargo using an airline, it will be very important to know how they each handle the cargo and what differences exist. Many passenger airlines are dependent upon the revenues they gain from moving cargo along with passengers and baggage. The netted crates and/or aluminum containers you see being loaded and off-loaded at passenger terminals is cargo material (see Figures 1.5 and 1.6). Passenger flights provide a wide choice of scheduling selection, since they are based on passenger routes and schedules. All-cargo flights are scheduled only two or three times a week, since they only move cargo.

Figure 1.5 Netted airline cargo configuration.

There is another offering by the all-cargo industry called charter flights, and these present several options for the use of charters by clients. Primarily, these involve the volume of cargo being moved by a client. Some client material is mass-produced and needs to be delivered to a region for either a critical phase of production or for a

Figure 1.6 Skid and pallet example.

customer obligation. You often see charters used when there is a roll-out of a new product. The product needs to be placed into inventory at the time and place(s) of the rollout when the new product launches. Since PAX flights can have limited space and all-cargo flights have limited scheduling as well as obligations to deliver materials for other clients, a client will sometimes charter an all-cargo aircraft. Most airlines have planes available for this use. Also, from a security perspective, these types of airships require special attention for a couple of reasons. One is due to the unpredictable timetables that can occur. The other is that the goods can easily be of high value and a security risk, such as computers or cell phones. It goes without saying both opportunistic and organized criminals target these commodities.

As a segment of the supply chain, material can be handed off to an airline at virtually any point—at or near the origin or all the way to the destination. Air transport can play a role on a regional level or at the intercontinental level. It is not unusual for goods to be transferred by trucking that was picked up directly from the client source to an airline. It is then flown to another regional or international airport, and then transported within this airport and handed off to another airline for a flight to yet another destination. Here, it is most likely handed off to a trucking provider, then moved to a customer or distribution center/provider. These inter-airport handoffs are of particular concern for security, since they occur behind airport gates with limited access by the security manager, which we discuss in the next section.

1.9 Third-Party Logistics Providers

Third-party logistics providers (3pls) are often inserted into the supply chain either by the client or by another service provider. The most common are either distribution centers (DCs) or freight forwarders, both of which operate differently. The DC is an operation that will take in materials or goods for a client and run a warehousing, sorting, knitting, or other handling or product/material manipulation for a client. Many companies use these providers as a cost and operational savings measure so that the associated costs do not affect their direct operating expense, since they are contracted out to a third party. Labor issues are also borne by the provider and not the product company. In most cases, these contracted providers receive and ship the client's goods, but they do not transport them to or from origins and destinations.

When a client contracts or arranges with another party for the transportation of goods through the supply chain, this function is in the realm of freight forwarding. These providers have a network of contacts and other transportation providers, such as airlines, trucking, and ocean carriers. The forwarder will work with the client regarding where and when the goods are to be picked up and delivered, and then make the necessary connections to make that happen.

As distribution centers, the 3pls act as fulfillment centers. They store, sort, and ship according to orders received by the client or the client's customers. Both contract warehousing and DC operations need a customized security plan for the prevention of theft and infiltration during all the handling and storage within the confines of the center or warehouse.

In some cases, the forwarder only makes the arrangements and does not actually handle any of the material. Others have their own warehouse, handling, and trucking operations that take in the cargo, redistribute it according to routes that are required by the customer, and then hand it off to other transport providers for delivery to destinations. The forwarders usually do not store the goods for long periods of time. They make their money by moving the cargo. Forwarding operations also require a unique security scheme, since the cargo is moving quickly and is handled by a number of people within the operation. There are several viable methods for the protection of goods and product moving through this link of the supply chain, which we address in the next section.

1.10 PODs

The proof of delivery (POD) is a very important function in the supply chain, as it is used to track the movement, location, and condition of goods and material at any given time. A POD is tied to the handoff. At each handoff, there is an exchange or transfer of goods and material, and with them comes the requisite paperwork provided by the client, transportation provider, government officials, and/or customer expecting the arrival of the goods. Integral with the handoff is an acknowledgement of the release by one provider to the care and custody of another. With the exchange is a sign-off, either electronically or (still most often) on paper, of all the information on the material—content, condition, and quality—and an acknowledgement by the receiving provider of the same information. This is the point where a good security program inspects the condition of the cargo and requires receivers to carefully document on the POD any and all conditions, good or bad, of the material (see Figure 1.7.)

Some clients require that all handoff PODs are to be sent back to them as they occur for verification and tracking. Others collect all of this information at the end of the chain once the cargo is delivered to the requested destination.

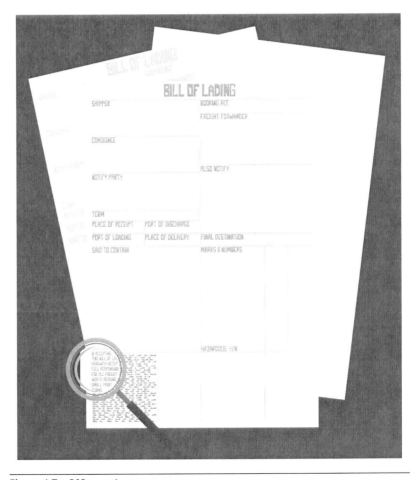

Figure 1.7   POD example.

2

ELEMENTS THAT IMPACT THE SUPPLY CHAIN

There are many hands that touch material while it passes through the supply chain. As a security professional, what should be keeping you awake at night is the security of the material—or, rather, considering the question, "Are any of these hands dirty?" The larger or greater the chain, so grows the number of hands manipulating the material for that particular service provider, as we discussed in Chapter 1.

In this chapter we will explore and examine all those not-so-proverbial hands and the many functions that these elements play in the security and operation of the supply chain. You will see not only the practical "hands," but also some of the important intangible activities and conditions that affect the chain.

Securing the supply chain takes a full understanding of the chain, as we have discussed. It also requires that you know where you are positioned to view that chain. In other words, where are you situated in relation to your client's relationship to the chain? Is it within the chain? Are you external to the chain? Are you a transportation provider, a third-party logistics provider (3pls), or possibly as support to insurance or risk management? Each one of these has a different perspective, standpoint, and interest toward the chain. You must be sure to align your security program and its function to those interests, based on your position and relationship to the supply chain.

As with the functional components of the supply chain, here you also need to see and understand many of the functions that can generally operate behind the curtain. They are equally important considerations of your supply chain security program. It also goes further into the integration of your security program, into the fabric of the company and/or client's objectives.

A single item can mean many things to many people. Part of your security function will be to know how each one uses that term (or

Figure 2.1　Representative skid.

function) and what it is that they think it requires from a security perspective. A simple example is the term pallet, which you see used all the time in the logistics world. However, some use the term pallet to mean skid. A skid and a pallet are not necessarily the same thing, however, the terms are used and understood interchangeably. A skid is a device that supports material when a forklift is applied for movement from one position to another. They are usually about 1.2 meters square and generally made of wood or plastic. A pallet can support or hold a larger amount of material or even several "skids" of material (see Figure 2.1). You may think of this as semantics, but when a client uses the term *pallet*, the client might also mean that the device is holding more than just an amount on a "skid." When tracking amounts of material when there is a loss or pilferage, the amount on the pallet can be very important. You can see that, in this way, you can speak your client's language in your client interactions and be precise in the development of your security protocol or program.

As a supply chain security planner, you might need to look into the client's business of how they produce or procure materials that they later entrust to you. If you are developing security at this early stage, look into how the client secures their own material prior to being placed into your care and the supply chain. Are they concerned about security? Do they have their own internal security program? Are they required to be compliant with a security regulation or government-sponsored supply chain security program or protocol? Are they complying? You may not be able to be allowed "behind the curtain" of a client; however, these are things to note when you take security control of their material. Once you take control, you can very well be held responsible for the client's security deficiencies. All too often, losses and thefts discovered down the line could have happened long before you can exert any control over the material.

2.1 Operations

The function of operations will be examined from the perspective of what your company or client may actually perform in or do for the supply chain. Some companies contract out nearly all of the necessary functions required for their business. This runs from using third parties for material development or acquisition, through manufacturing, to transportation, and the delivery to end users.

Knowing this operational position will predicate your approach to security. For a subcontract position, where your client/company relies heavily on contractual relationships and services, you have the task of attempting to incorporate your security plan into the current security functions (or lack thereof) with the particular subcontracted provider. Many providers have security programs that fit their requirements or are designed with compliance to local or federal law regulations. Very often, we see that their security programs are effective and go a long way in the protection of your client's material. This is a happy problem, but one that still needs examination for compliance and competency. The more difficult situations are ones where you are confronted with noncompliance, lack of interest, or outright malfeasance.

A further impact that may prove to be a difficult task occurs when these suppliers and/or providers are situated globally instead of contained regionally. Besides mere distances, time zones, and language barriers, you will be dealing with a wide range of business cultures, global and regional company differences, as well as other influences imposed by national programs. You will find that skills of communication, negotiation, and comprehension come to the forefront when working to instill your security focus into another's domain.

2.2 Contracts

Contracts are the lifeblood of any organization. They stipulate, regulate, obligate, confirm, and clarify (plus a whole host of other legal and operational elements) the business relationship between one or more entities. Very often, this is a region that has not traditionally been on the security provider's radar screen. In fact, understanding the contract is one of the most important activities a security professional can do for the client. Additionally, being involved in contract development should be a priority in the security model and business integration plan.

Nearly every element or clause of the contract between the client and their provider, supplier, or other business partner that is involved in the transportation, handling, storage, insurance/risk management, and protection of a client's material or products should be closely examined by security. Much of the contract is indeed composed of descriptions of services, but there is also language of liability and other obligations for the protection of the material against loss, theft, or other security-related events. We have seen many contracts that do not even address any security concerns or approach the design of a plan to protect the material or product from loss, tampering, or theft. Often, these events are covered under blanket risk management or insurance-related OS&D (overages, shortages, and damage) clauses. This is a critical area where security must be involved to understand what programs or plans might be in place, or the lack thereof, that can impact the security of the material. Depending upon how these clauses are structured, OS&D claims can directly impact the bottom line of a company. Losses might be paid out of a fund, from insurance premiums, or even from shareholders. In just about every case, the loss or theft of product hurts the bottom line either from the point of lost revenue, increased direct operating expense (DOE), duplication of effort, increased insurance premiums, lost customers, and/or tarnished brand recognition.

In order to effect a competent review of contracts for security issues, the security professional must also be knowledgeable in the other aspects of the business involved in the relationship. One of the most important is risk management and insurance. Here again, it depends upon how a company might structure its own business units (BUs). Security professionals need to have an understanding of how that internal body functions, as it enables them to view contracts and agreements with a broader understanding and a lens with which to recognize potential threats to the products or materials and, in the end, to the company's financial well-being.

There are a number of well-used terms that could potentially impact your client's liability and financial position, such as *force majeure, negligence, gross negligence, care and custody, lack of care, Warsaw Pact,* etc. This is not a study in risk management or law, but it is very important for security to see how these types of terms are utilized in relationship to the protection or loss of their material. Without a security plan in place, there is the potential that any loss, theft, pilferage, or shortage could negatively impact your client. You may not be able to recover any loss from a supplier or provider in the event of a loss if certain critical language is not in place or applied appropriately.

Security must ensure that there is appropriate language inserted into the contract, either within existing clauses or articles, or having its own title or heading. This is where a clear security plan will be spelled out, understood, and agreed by all parties. We will talk more on this in Chapter 5.

2.3 Customer Demands, Written and Nonwritten

We will expand here from the previous section. From the perspective of being a customer of a provider: They provide the service for you, the customer. Let us look at it from the opposing view, where you are the provider for your customer. Here you do not own the material. Even though you might have it in your possession, title of the material has not been passed to you. For a period of time, you merely handle the product. It was handed to you, and at some point you will hand it off to another. Or in the case of some providers, e.g., transportation, you might be charged with accessing, contracting, and monitoring other providers for your customer as specified in an agreement or contract with them for your services.

The security relationship is obviously different. Now you are the one who must view the material as your own and devise and develop effective security plans, or you receive a security plan from your customer for the protection of the material, and need to implement that plan according to your agreement with them. You can start to see here the potential conflicts posed to security. Are the customer's security demands in sync with your own internal plans? Is the customer security plan even valid and applicable? Is there a cost to you? Or them? Or both? Are there any conflicts with governmental regulations on your end?

The importance of having a defined, agreed upon, and written security program with the customer is paramount. As discussed previously, certain contractual language determines the elements of obligation and liability. You need to know these prior to receiving the material. You need to know these as you determine and contract with other providers, if that is part and parcel to your overall agreement with the customer. Knowing these obligations also reveals your potential exposure to liability in the financial sense, as in risk management/insurance liabilities.

Be aware of the unwritten obligations and liabilities. It is not unusual for customer not to have any security plans for their material. When receiving material from a customer, there are certain assumed responsibilities for its care while in your custody. These can often be expanded to being liable for issues with the other providers that you had identified and utilized for the handling and/or transportation of the customer's products. Some customers make an assumption from their side that you have a viable security program in place that incorporates the care and protection of their products while in your custody. Other customers feel that, since you have received the product, you will be the one to develop and implement a security plan for the entire time the material is in your custody and for any other provider you have identified. Amazingly, even customers who are involved in the manufacture or distribution of high-value, high-risk products can hand off that material to others with no perceptible security plan in place. Here again, there could be an assumption that your plan is sufficient to protect this product and cargo from thieves attracted to its high value and desirability. Failure to provide this protection might be an issue of contention in the event of a loss. Here again, the issue of who pays for a loss and what language was (or not) in place to address that issue comes up.

While there are some basic care and custody liabilities applicable, it is the interpretation of the elements of any event that has occurred that impacted the customer material that can be the most challenging situation. When anything is left open to interpretation, the true conditions and facts becomes cloudy. Re-creating these conditions through investigation and other methods may not be possible, and settlement of claims and issues can take months to years.

This is another pitch for your security program to be fully integrated into your client's or company's business. There should be regular and continual contact with the functions of risk management and the legal department, among others, to keep yourself and your security program knowledgeable, germane, and current.

2.4 Provider Capability

While on the subject of providers, let us also look at their capability from the perspective of security. Look to see if there is a security program, with defined procedures and protocols. Further, is there a security structure with identifiable security management and contacts locally, regionally, or globally? There could be all, part, or none of these security features in place. Suppliers and providers are in the business of offering their particular product for a reasonable fee while retaining as much gross profit as possible. Having an integrated security plan is not always a priority. Security is often viewed as an expense, not as a revenue generator. Therefore, some profit and loss (P&L) plans do not address specific security programs. Rather, security is blended into the day-to-day practices for normal care and custody handling. Liabilities can also be blended into their OS&D risk and insurance programs. Security concerns of loss, theft, pilferage, etc., are only part of the mix and not given priority or explicit attention.

This not to say that the provider is unable to provide a viable security program; it is to say that they do not view it as a priority. When you deal with a provider in this category, it will be important to look into the operations of the provider and see how security is actually incorporated into their business. If your company hands off low-risk, low-value material such as trash cans to a provider, worrying about the provider's security program might be unnecessary.

However, handling high-value, high-risk material such as computer chips, electronics, or pharmaceuticals is a different story. As the security representative for your client, you have the obligation to ensure that (a) the providers who handle this material have effective security programs in place and (b) that these programs are given the priority, attention, and requisite training for implementation for the protection of your material. As you scrutinize the provider's security, you can determine whether they even have the capacity to arrange for your security demands. There could be lack of interest, personnel, training, funding, or overall expertise, any one of which would inhibit an effective program. Sometimes, these conditions can be corrected. Sometimes they cannot, possibly based on the provider's internal structure and ability. In such cases, you may be forced to work with the provider to develop a security program, look into cost sharing, and possibly, in extreme circumstances, look to use another provider who better fits your required security plan.

2.5 Geography

As your client's product travels through the supply chain, it will also travel across the land, sea, or air of any locale, region, country, or continent at any given time. These topographical references impact the supply chain by way of travel time, distance, environment, and weather conditions. They can also influence the way your material is handled or stored. An example to consider is material that is handled in temperate zones, where it may often be stored outside of traditional warehouses or, if not outside, then in open-sided buildings with little or no dock door coverage, screening, or gates. In some countries where the transportation infrastructure is not well developed, material that is required to travel over long distances may be handed off several times as it traverses plains, rivers, or mountainous regions. This is good to know, especially if your product could be a target for theft.

2.6 Force Majeure/Acts of God

According to Wikipedia:[1]

> *Force majeure* [French]…or *vis major* (Latin) "superior force," also known as *cas fortuit* (French) or *casus fortuitus* (Latin) "chance occurrence, unavoidable accident," is a common clause in contracts that essentially frees both parties from liability or obligation when an extraordinary event or circumstance beyond the control of the parties, such as a war, strike, riot, crime, or an event described by the legal term *act of God* (such as hurricane, flooding, earthquake, volcanic eruption, etc.), prevents one or both parties from fulfilling their obligations under the contract.

In this section, we are going to look at force majeure as an element that impacts the supply chain. The main reason is that, with all the security planning for the protection of cargo and material in the supply chain, we often forget that there are other noncriminal-based influences that can have a direct impact where security still needs to be involved. Many companies look to address these types of events under contingency planning, crisis management, or business-continuity planning programs. Many of these plans require operations to build programs that prepare for the event and attempt to mitigate any associated impacts (e.g., personal injuries, structural damage, business disruption, communications, file storage, etc.).

From a corporate standpoint, security would be involved in the development of these plans. From a supply chain viewpoint, security should be looking at how the product would be impacted—not so much as damage by wind or water or something of that nature, but from exposing the product to vulnerability through theft, pilferage, or tampering. In-house security protocols would be part of the company's business continuity planning (BCP). However, what about when the material is already in the supply chain and being handled by a provider? How will your security program deal with this contingency?

There are a few things to consider when developing your supply chain security-contingency program. First, know your suppliers and providers. Know who they are and specifically where they would be controlling or handling your product at any given point in time. Second, have a communications plan. Have a firm contact with these providers, both on a corporate level and at each location you have identified as handling your material. Third, examine their contingency programs to identify any potential gaps that would place your product at peril.

2.7 Crime

The generally accepted crime triangle model is: opportunity, ability, and desire or motive[2] (see Figure 2.2). Their order is not important. For a theft to occur, these three sides of the triangle must be connected. Take away any one, and it falls apart. *Opportunity* can be described as being at the right place at the right time. It would be like finding a lock unlocked. This would offer the opportunity for an illegal entry that would not have existed if the lock were properly fastened and locked.

The next would be *ability*. Using the lock scenario, an open lock presents the opportunity; the ability would involve opening the door and removing the targeted goods, or even the ability to place oneself at the unlocked door. Ability is not a hard-and-fast definition. It can also be viewed as having the capacity or capability to commit the crime. A simplistic example would be a bulky target, such as a 60" TV, which you cannot simply pick up. If you did not bring a lift or a cart or another person to help carry it, you leave. The theft does not occur.

The third side to the triangle is *desire* or *motive*—the why. You are looking to take or steal or acquire the goods for your own use or gain. Here, you want to steal a TV to convert it to cash; you know where it is; you go to the container; the lock is open, and you take

Figure 2.2 Crime triangle.

the TV. There has been a theft. On a social level, there could be a discussion of what motivates people to commit crimes. However, speaking strictly of the elements of crime: The desire drives the act; the opportunity places the proceeds in reach; and the ability allows the crime to be fulfilled.

A review of crime statistics for the United States will easily support the idea that you will need to protect your goods from those who look to relieve you of them. According to FBI crime statistics, the United States experienced a reported $30 billion in theft losses in 2010. These losses are a total of all reported theft, but this number illustrates the broad range of theft losses. Cargo crime, specifically, has only been tracked since 1990, and the data reveal a steady increase year by year since then.[3]

Crime in any region or country should be looked at as one more type of environment that your goods and products would be exposed to while traveling through the supply chain pipeline. It is not all that dissimilar to weather or handling circumstances. Crime, when looked at as a force, is out there, constantly seeking to exploit a weak spot, one little crack in the armor, a kink in the chain.

Crime comes in many forms and can occur at any location, at any time, on any day. This is no secret, of course. However, unless you, as the security professional, keep this relentless condition in the forefront with your company and providers, it can take a back seat to the regular business at hand. When little or nothing bad happens, customers, companies, and providers can fall into a false sense of security. After being in this industry even for a short time, you will hear the comments: "If nothing happens, then why do we need all that security?" "If there is no crime in my neighborhood, then why do we need all these police here?" "If I have not been experiencing theft, loss, or pilferages with my goods in the supply chain, then why are we pushing for more security training and programs?"

Try this for a response: "Are you willing to drop or remove the security program surrounding this material, and see what happens? Crime will still be out there, but we will not be there to stop it." A drop in crime—a reduction in theft and pilferage—does not happen by accident. Hardening the target against the criminal element is a primary method to keep your products safe and secure. However, to say that you are the only one who has effected this resilience would be a fallacy. The reality is that it takes any number of programs, policies, and protocols as well as well-trained people to implement and monitor these security practices.

Another important fact that your company and your client should know is that crime is not only an "external" force. The wolf at the door that is trying to get in is not your only worry. It is estimated that nearly 85% of all thefts involve inside information.[4] Such information can include sensitive knowledge regarding your materials. Go back and review some of the most well-known publicized thefts. They all have one thing in common: The thieves had some level of inside information passed to them from an internal source. This information enabled them to learn important facts that were then exploited to commit the crime. This information could be any one fact or a combination of facts and circumstances. For instance:

- Physical location of the target material
- Security conditions of the containment of the material
- Timing of any guarding
- Alarm systems in place
- Alarm codes
- CCTV (closed-circuit television) systems in place
- Transport modes and methods while in transit

The list can go on and on. We will discuss this later, but for now, there is another extremely important piece of armor that can be put into place when building your supply chain security program: qualified and vetted personnel. Most cases of inside information come from those whom you trust the most. It comes from the people you have hired to handle, manage, transport, and protect the products while moving through your portion of the supply chain. What makes it worse is that it can come not only from your people. It can come from people within your suppliers and providers anywhere along the chain. Don't forget origin and destination people, either. This brings in your developers and initial material resources, your end users, and your customers. It is almost like trying to explain the universe. What I mean is that attacks can come from anywhere; the sources of these instigators are virtually boundless. Information on your material that is of value to thieves can come from anywhere, inside or outside of your organization.

Various types of criminals may try to prey upon your supply chain. The basic archetypes of criminals include opportunists, professionals, terrorists, predators, and masters.[5] How these criminal types target your supply chain depends on their individual motivations and perceived outcomes. The least likely might be the opportunists, as they generally take advantage of a perceived gap in your security program and seize that opportunity for what they feel they can gain in the short term. This means that you must continually audit and review your security measures to ensure that your locks are always locked. The others are more troublesome. They will, according to their own methodology, attack your goods in a planned and deliberate fashion.

Anything you can do to disrupt or block their plan to separate you from your goods could take away one of those legs of the crime triangle. For the criminal to be successful in thefts from the supply chain, several "transactions" must occur: planning, theft activity, supply and demand considerations, fencing, distribution, and evaluation of risk versus reward.[6] Evaluation involves the outcome, where they either enjoy the fruits of their labor or, hopefully, spend time behind bars: Was it worth it? In the absence of positive outcomes, the desire for criminal activity is diminished, as there may not be any returns for the effort. You may be able to directly influence only some of these components. However, the more successful you are in deterrence or prevention, the less successful the criminal becomes.

We have looked at the professional criminal approach, which involves obtaining pertinent internal information about your organization, your products, and your security capabilities. And then there are the opportunists, who are always out there.

Remember the crime-triangle model. Criminals seek an opportunity or prospect of succeeding in their particular criminal act. These criminals may be searching for that opportunity, cruising by, watching and waiting for a gap or a lack of security in your operations. Or they may develop their opportunity by working to gain general knowledge of the circumstances surrounding your product. This would not necessarily be protected inside or internal information; it could also be public information, readily available to anyone. Such information might also be obtained through deliberate observation, research, and surveillance. Once sufficient information is gathered and the criminals are able to detect or observe a weakness, they will use that insight to attack the target. This attack is not necessarily a violent attack, although that can never be ruled out. Armed hijackings, warehouse invasions, kidnappings, and armed burglaries are common. Armed attacks are more prevalent in some regions than others (which should be part of your review of the environment where your goods are housed or transported). An additional concern is to how to plan for such a contingency. An armed or violent attack adds the factor of injury or death to your personnel, and this must be incorporated into your security training program.

Speaking from an opportunist angle, the criminals are working off of information they developed, which can be flawed. Once the attack goes into action, they might be faced with a situation they had not anticipated, complicating their plan and placing your organization at great risk. They may very well retreat, knowing things are not as they planned, or they may overreact and push through, attempting to force a desired outcome.

2.8 Volume

The word *volume* refers to the amount of goods, cargo, material, etc., that populates the space within the supply chain. Depending on the industry, these volumes could be stated in terms of pounds or kilos; liquid measures; cubic feet, yards, or meters; or possibly as numbers of pieces, cartons, crates, skids or something of that nature. Be sure to know how your company or client views their own volumes.

Knowing the descriptions and actual amounts associated with their volume will help to give a sense of how much of the company's material you will be watching over in your supply chain security program. It is safe to assume that watching over a few pieces or kilos of material would be easier than watching over a constant flow of hundreds or thousands of pieces or pounds of products. Volume is also important to understand when dealing with your providers or suppliers. Do they have the physical capacity to handle the amount of material you present to them? Maybe they do, or maybe they find a way, but does it compromise their internal security program or yours for your client? Providers often take on more than they can handle because it represents revenue for them. When faced with overloads, they seek other subcontracted suppliers to take on the extra volume. Sometimes this is for the short term, the long term, or it can be a regular method of doing business. If this occurs, do these subcontracts then carry out their (or your) agreed-upon security program? Do they have the ability to provide this security? There is a lot to contemplate.

Another contingency for your supply chain security program is its ability to expand or contract according to need or, in terms of this section, the volume at any point in time. Add to this situation the complicating factor of protecting high-value or high-risk goods. Protecting a few high-risk pieces is one plan; protecting hundreds of kilos of the same product is a different situation. Volume plus value/ risk is an important combination to be included when compiling your plan.

2.9 Storage Capacity

Directly related to volume is storage capacity, which briefly deserves extra attention. We talked previously about whether a provider had the ability to handle the volume of your material. Then, in turn, does their subcontractor (if utilized) have the ability? Storage is a concept for the provider. It involves physical dimensions of space, but it also involves their ability to transfer the volume into their internal systems, track it with accuracy, and, when called upon, produce the material in good condition in a time, place, and manner as requested by the customer.

You must carefully examine your providers for their ability to accept, contain, and protect your material. As we previously defined, as a component of the supply chain, there are contract logistics providers who handle your material in warehouse settings for general storage or who produce added values such as distribution or "pick-n-pack."

When examining these providers, you must question whether they demonstrate that they have total accountability, control, and security over the goods at all times. Inventory control and other logistics accounting methods are standard processes. Security needs to fully comprehend these storage-related processes to better determine if there are gaps that can expose vulnerability to pilferage or shortages due to loss or "shrinkage."

2.10 Government Controls

The entire supply chain operates under the scrutiny, inspection, or general regulatory environment of one form of government agency or another. Further, there are overlapping jurisdictions, prerogatives, programs, etc., where a company operating within the chain, or sending goods into and through it, have a variety of governmental influences and reports that demand compliance. These governmental organizations control tariffs, import and export reports, labor, permits, bills of lading, manifests, and even the security of goods, services, people, and transport.

Government controls exist at all levels and in all segments of the supply chain, and the security of the supply chain must consider them and, in many cases, ensure compliance. Every state, country, and region of the globe has one or more programs reigning over the supply chain. In Chapter 7 we will examine in more detail some of the government controls that exert their impact over the supply chain. Currently, however, the important object to remember is that security of the supply chain also has to be built around measures over which you have little or no control. Lack of knowledge or dismissal of these programs can lead to negative consequences. Companies and providers who operate with the supply chain on a daily basis are well aware of these programs and often have a compliance function to monitor and ensure government compliance for their organization. Since these programs can and do affect security, the compliance function should be aligned with the security function. This provides insight into the government controls and their ever-changing influence. It also allows security to adjust its program or to be aware if there are security protocols that might interfere with a regulation.

References

1. www.wikipedia.com.
2. Marcus Felson, *Crime and Everyday Life: Insight and Implications for Society* (Thousand Oaks, CA: Pine Forge Press, 1994).
3. FBI, "Inside Cargo Theft: A Growing, Multi-Billion-Dollar Problem," *FBI Stories*, November 12, 2010, http://www.fbi.gov/news/stories/2010/november/cargo_111210/cargo_111210.
4. *Cargo Security News*, "Cargo Theft in the Transportation Industry," Transport Security—Enforcer Cargo Security Intelligence Center, April 15, 2011, http://www.transportsecurity.com/blog/template_archives_cat.asp?cat=31.
5. Russ Alan Prince, "The Criminal Mind," *Financial Advisor*, August 2008, http://www.fa-mag.com/component/content/article/38-features/4758-the-criminal-mind-augsept08.html.
6. Marilyn Walsh and Duncan Chappell, "Operational Parameters in the Stolen Property System," chap. 12 in *Crime Types: A Text Reader* (Belmont, CA: Thompson Wadsworth, 2004).

3

SECURITY

Supply Chain versus Corporate

There is a noticeable difference between supply chain security and the traditional corporate security that many security professionals support. We will examine some of these differences to help show that many companies rely on the corporate security function to oversee supply chain issues. Experience has shown that not only are there some fundamental program differences and foci, but also that what the organization expects from them can be diverse and even divergent.

3.1 Focus of the Program

According to ASIS International, corporate security can generally be defined as the organizational function responsible for providing "comprehensive, integrated risk strategies (policy, procedures, management, training, etc.) to help protect an organization from security threats."[1]

The primary focus of such a program is the protection of the core business: the "parent." Depending upon the industry involved (i.e., finance, IT [information technology] services, manufacturing, etc.), the core competency of the organization may have very specific and real threats to consider. The more well known IT security is, these hacking and other attacks for fun and profit are a constant threat. A corporation in this industry would primarily focus its security expertise on these threats. In finance, the threat would be fraud. No matter what the industry, a well-rounded security program will be designed to protect the core as well as the support mechanisms that enable the organization to function and operate. Corporate security would also concern itself with personnel security, building and perimeter security, visitor identification and monitoring, incoming packages and mail, etc.

Supply chain security, as a corporate or organizational function, could be somewhat different from traditional corporate security. For the security professional who is charged with protecting goods and material utilizing the supply chain, it is important to analyze and understand the function of security for that organization. It is also important to know whether the organization views security as a corporate "core protector" or if they desire a more specialized approach, such as directing a primary security focus on a specified function or task, e.g., a supply chain service. Additionally, this focus should be identified for your own internal needs, such as budgeting and other resources, and for when you must interact with other participants in the supply chain. You should look to see whether the suppliers, providers, and contractors handling or controlling your material have a focus of security on those tasks or whether they are looking at security in the corporate approach. Some corporations and companies ask security to perform both. However, others do not make this connection for one reason or another, which is what you need to know.

3.2 Corporate Culture

Besides the business need for security—whether to protect people, places, and things, or for compliance to internal and external programs—how does the security function fit within the corporate culture of the organization? The internal culture or operational environment of a group is the result of a combination of the values and characteristics that define an organization. It has a direct impact and influence on the way employees specifically and the organization as a whole relate to each other, to customers, to shareholders, and to business partners. It drives behaviors and unites employees around a shared set of values.[2] These values can be good or bad, positive or negative, supportive or destructive, or any combination thereof. A well-integrated and performing security program produces positive *externalities*.[3] This is the indirect or collateral impact of the program. An externality of a proper supply chain security program is a hardening of the target. Evildoers do not see opportunities to gain illicit access to the material, so they move to another, softer target. You will not be able to stop crime. All you need to worry about is that your company or client will not fall victim to it; let them steal from some other company.

For a security professional, the questions are: "Is security a corporate value?" "Does the culture of this organization value security?" "Is security integrated into the corporate culture, or is it merely a required office or even a vexation?" Answering these questions will help you to place your security function on the hierarchy of needs for your company or client. And, when dealing with those suppliers and providers, you need to ask, "Where is security within their corporate culture?"

3.3 Supplier and Provider Relationships

When reviewing corporate versus supply chain security, we stated that there is a question to be answered in reference to the positioning of security within the organizations of your suppliers and providers. What is the focus of their security program? Where is it in their hierarchy or list of priorities? This could also include going as far back into origin as to evaluate security in the context of resource procurement or manufacturing of your goods, products, and material. If they work your material, then you should be concerned and examine their programs and culture. If your company or client does not take title to the material, you should also be concerned and aware, since there could be a government supply chain security program regulating or reviewing your materials. We will examine these issues in Chapter 8 to emphasize that your security assessment should be comprehensive to include these entities. With regard to risk management or insurance, issues with these entities prior to taking title may limit or remove liability for losses and theft. However, not to involve them in your supply chain security review could leave a significant gap that could be exploited or detected later when you do have possession or title.

References

1. ASIS International Standards Committee, "Chief Security Officer (CSO) Organizational Standard," ASIS International, (Alexandria, VA, 2008).
2. *Human Resource Management* 44, no. 1 (2005): 79–84.
3. Steven D. Levitt and Stephen J. Dubner, *SuperFreakonomics* (New York: HarperCollins, 2009).

PART II

DEVELOPING A SUPPLY CHAIN SECURITY PROGRAM

4

SECURITY FOR KEY LINKS IN THE CHAIN

Now that we have scrutinized the many links, relationships, and functions of a traditional supply chain, we will now move into the development and applications of very specific security measures for key links in the supply chain. Security for a supply chain must concern itself with the known and the unknown. The known includes the actual functions of the segments of the supply chain. The known is also the operating conditions in the environments where the particular supply chain segments are employed. You know how your warehouse works; you know how your goods are transported; you know how others handle and hand off your goods. Knowing these activities enables you to build a fairly stable and uniform security program to respond to the relative constants you have identified. The unknowns are the myriad influences and forces that exist within the very same environments where your goods are being handled and stored. And, even though you endeavor to anticipate their impact, you are not certain about where, when, and how they will decide to test your security systems, protocols, and procedures. The unknown calls for contingency planning as an essential ingredient in your overall security program.

For this second section of our supply chain security book, we will drop the higher level descriptive approach in favor of a more detailed and practical approach for the prescribed security actions you will need to understand and consider while developing your security plan.

4.1 Origin

Remember that origin, for the most part, is where the material or goods you own or control first enter the supply chain. We will start our security program there. The first action is to perform a full and detailed security audit of this origin operation. This is needed whether it is a factory, supplier, or other resource provider. Look at all their security resources and how those resources are acclimated to protect your products. Appendix A has an example of a security review and audit. You must ensure that all the security needs of your material are covered. This may mean that you can take a template security audit or devise one of your own, but it is to be formulated or customized for your specific needs.

4.1.1 Security Reviews of Origin

It is important that, at this juncture of reviewing origin, we examine the security audit function for origins. When performing these reviews, do them in person on site(s) or have a trusted and experienced security professional perform the task. Do not rely on the supplier, provider, or factory to "self-assess." By self-assessment, we mean that you contact the location or operation and request that they perform a security review based on the direction or form and format that you provide for them. Self-assessments are notoriously inaccurate. The inaccuracy manifests itself in poor quality or detail, erroneous or false data, and lack of depth and content when describing past or current security issues. The list goes on.

These inaccuracies are caused by any number of reasons. There can be a refusal to perform the review, citing that they have their own internal review and that they either will forward what they feel should be reported or possibly report nothing at all. Some organizations refuse to share this type of information, claiming that the information is proprietary and not for release. This may not be an issue if the operation is controlled or owned by your client, but in cases of contract work, it might be a concern. In these instances, at the time of the development of the agreement or contract with these suppliers, it would be very important to include your security requirements along with an additional requirement of security review or audit reporting. The language in the agreement should allow for you, or your representative, to perform an on-site review with open access to the entire facility and to any and all security-related data, files, personnel, and equipment.

Other inaccuracies resulting from self-assessment could come from the fact that the local operations person assigned to complete the review is not experienced in security and does not fully understand the security function. Some organizations have a local person identified as their "security manager" or someone of that sort. The question then will be, "Is that person performing security in title only?" This will need to be determined before allowing this local person to file the security report.

Another source of inaccurate results comes from the culture of the operation. This would include deliberate skewing or manipulation of the security self-reporting. Management may try to tamper with the security review in order to ensure that it bathes the operation in a positive light. These concerns by management may stem from a fear that a poor security review would cause unwanted attention from higher levels of management, or pose a risk for customers who could, in turn, choose to withdraw their business. Another underlying cause might be financial. If the security review reveals security gaps, a resulting action plan would involve programs and actions to close those gaps. New or revised security measures may be required. These measures easily could have a cost associated with them. Increasing DOE (direct operating expenses) and other expenses that could negatively impact the P&L (profit and loss) statement of an operation could drive a manager to influence a security review to reflect more positively. You may see yourself needing to draw upon your negotiation and diplomatic skills if you detect this attitude or sense resistance from the origin operation.

4.2 Actions

The origin operation needs to fully understand the threats and vulnerabilities of your material and also recognize what gaps you have detected. Do not be surprised if origin takes issue with your findings. They could be defensive for a perceived lack of security attention on their part, or they could be self-justifying of their current program, especially if there have been few security issues in the past. Your security review is established for *your* material and not for other customers or clients they might handle. If origin is dedicated to or owned/operated by your client or company, then instilling a requisite security plan will be difficult. In the case of suppliers, contractors, or providers, there will be competing interests from other individual companies. In this last case, even though your proposed security plan might overlap existing security measures in place by the provider, your primary task is to have your additional essential procedures and protocols expressed and implemented.

Another reason to place an inordinate amount of security attention on origin is that this is the point in your supply chain where the condition and presentation of your goods are first documented and acknowledged. Without this first important step, it is near impossible to state with certainty what changes may have occurred if issues are later discovered farther down the supply chain. All descriptions of the material must be taken into account, such as

- Visual appearance
- Piece counts
- Weights
- Physical dimensions
- Condition of wrapping and exterior coverings
- Temperatures (if applicable to the products)

All of this documentation must be taken in several forms. A digital still or video camera is mandatory. It stores visual information that can be easily transmitted anywhere and to anyone. Accurate and complete paperwork or manifests, bills of lading (BOLs), government forms, as well as required internal company paperwork and forms must be fully completed. There is always a temptation to minimize the documentation either from workload or laziness. However, it must be done properly, completely, and in its entirety. You cannot go back into time; neither can you go back into origin and validate conditions and dimensions (DIMs) if it is not done in the first place.

4.3 Customers

If your function and relationship with the supply chain involves the storage, handling, or movement of a customer's goods, then your security program might take a slightly different tack. Your customer, hopefully, will be coming to you with a security plan for their goods. If not, your additional responsibility would be to develop a viable plan for them, even if they do not request it or internalize it for current or future use when dealing with your client or company. Your security procedures for the customer's material will consist of three elements.

The first is an understanding of their material. What kind of material is it? What does it consist of? What conditions or specialized handling might it require due to its composition and components? Second, what security risk will it be exposed to while in your care? Does this material have a value for others? Is there a desired use by those other than your customer? Does it possess an elevated monetary value if it ends up in the hands of others? Are there components such as precious or semiprecious metals involved? And third, what appropriate counteractions, protocols, procedures, and plans must be in place for the protection of the material, while in your care, that will mitigate the risk and harden the target?

Appendix B provides examples of security requirements that could be used for customer material. You will notice that some of these requirements are hard to justify and may not even be viable, depending upon geological, country, or regional location; expense versus loss risk; lack of available technology; or even governmental restrictions. Your job is to extract the applicable actions and implement them through compliance and training.

4.4 Providers

Contracting out services for the handling or transportation of your own or your customer's products adds another layer of difficulty to a supply chain security program. Not only are you focused on your own program; you also need to add each and every provider you contract with at each and every location where that provider will handle your goods. A single provider at a single location is quite manageable. However, the presence of multiple providers of multiple modes of handling and transportation, at multiple locations, develops into a complex matrix of security risks and vulnerabilities.

Figure 4.1 depicts how the scale of multiple providers and locations will affect your security program. When developing the security plan for your goods, applying a matrix will reveal the scope required for your security program. A single provider at a single location has minimum impact. Two or more providers at the same location have an impact, but their presence at a single location will add stability to your security program. Multiple locations compound the problem due to geographic location and distances as well as differences in regional

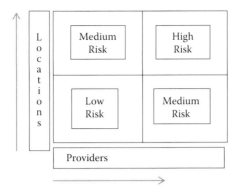

Figure 4.1   Risk elevator.

management, regulations, and culture. Developing and populating a matrix provides a method to identify and track the various handoff points and handlers as material passes though the supply chain.

The matrix should include

- Name of the provider
- Type of service or product offered or supplied
- Geographic address
- Location finder such as "Google Maps" depicting physical topographical location

You may find that you will be required to develop multiple databases for each route or lane of the supply chain you are covering. If different types of goods or materials use different types of providers, then it is advisable to build a separate matrix for each type. You may see that the same provider or supplier might be duplicated at some point, but there will be others that have their own unique relationship to your client's or company's material. An example is that two different types of material may come from the same origin, but are routed to destinations differently, with one using air and the other using ocean transport. Air and ocean transport providers have their own ground and handling processes and subsuppliers. The idea here is to follow and track your goods and know who is handling it and where, not to build a database of all your providers.

Once you have identified all suppliers and providers, then you can more easily track your tasks of contacting them, determining their security programs, and conducting security performance audits and reviews.

4.4.1 Provider Security Review

Performing a security review is imperative. It provides you with a good working knowledge of the services provided by your suppliers and providers, the way they service clients similar to you, and also how they service your material. The security review has two facets: procedural and practical. The procedural aspect involves the plan they use to protect your material. You will want to see their security manuals, protocols, and procedures. This would also include their crisis management as well as their disaster and business-continuity planning. These plans and documents must depict specific security-related actions that are in place. Knowing your products and understanding the provider's security procedures will highlight any security service gaps. From here, you can build an action plan to fill those gaps.

The other facet is the practical. These are the in-place security mechanisms that are designed and implemented to fulfill *your* security protocols and ensure compliance and documentation of their security programs for points and locations where they are handling *your* material. These involve concrete applications such as CCTV (closed-circuit television), access controls, alarms, lighting, etc.

4.4.2 CCTV

CCTV camera components must be of high-resolution digital quality and have the capacity of color for daylight and black and white for nighttime hours. There is a vast variety of camera types and applications on the market, so there is always an appropriate CCTV camera available. CCTV footage should be either continuous or motion activated. CCTV should be captured digitally or on servers and saved, at a minimum, for thirty days, with ninety days or longer being preferable. Determining the length of time to store CCTV footage is based upon two factors. The first is how long your providers or suppliers generally hold or handle your material. CCTV must cover your material for the entire length of stay at any given point or location. The second is the amount of time it takes for your material to pass through the supply chain to the end user at destination. Transit and handling times can range from days to weeks and even months if there are protracted storage points along the way.

CCTV documentation should be in place for a sufficient amount of time such that it will span the time needed to allow the material to reach the end user; allow the destination to inspect and document its condition, quality, and count; and allow for any discrepancies to be reported to your security-reporting platforms.

The length of delay from handling by a particular supplier to the point where a loss, theft, or other security issue can be reported to your security program determines the minimum amount of time that the supplier must keep the CCTV footage stored and available for review.

4.4.3 Access Controls

Your provider's access-control program should not be all that dissimilar to their CCTV program. Key access points, doors, and passages are to be controlled. The systems of control must be highly controlled, preferably utilizing an electronic mechanism such as proxy cards or swipe cards. Pushpin-type combination locks could be acceptable if the combination were changed regularly and limited only to those with need-to-know access. Keys—the most inexpensive option—are unfortunately also the most unreliable. Keys are easily duplicated and can be passed to others without detection. Keyed locks are rarely changed. Lost keys are always a concern. They also provide little documentation of use at the points of passing, entry, or exit.

The use of electronic devices documents the transit of people through passing points. Access cards are to be assigned to one person and not shared. This allows capture of the door/location, date, time, and person passing through a point of entry or exit. The data collected by the access-control system must be stored for the same amount of time as the CCTV system. Re-creating the conditions of a security incident or breach at a location relies on both CCTV and access control in an attempt to identify who had access to the material.

4.4.4 Intrusion Alarms

Some providers operate on a 7/24/365 basis. Many do not, instead operating closer to normal business hours and days. Even those who are 7/24 might have a closure for an occasional holiday or event. In any case, the security review for a provider must include a determination and inspection of their alarm systems. All external access points must be covered, including windows, doors, hatches, and any garage or roll-down doors or bays. Testing procedures must also be reviewed. An inspection of a provider location might also include rooftops and subterranean compartments. If a roof, basement, attached building, or room is breached, will it allow unauthorized access into the section of the provider location where your material is housed or handled? If so, then an applicable alarm detection device, such as motion detectors or glass-break/crash sensors, must be installed.

Another aspect of a provider alarm system is whether there is a backup system. Backup systems usually contain batteries or other power-storage devices that enable the alarm system to remain active in the event of a partial or complete power outage. However, this does not provide any alarm coverage or breach notification if communication lines to a control-reporting station are damaged or detached. When inspecting the alarm program of a provider location, take notice of this backup protocol and procedure. Trouble alarms—those that signal a break or malfunction of a line of communication in the alarms links—are only effective if they are detected and an effective response protocol is in place. The most effective backup systems are UPS (uninterrupted power source)-supported cellular backups. These backup systems afford constant communication links even when there are power failures; damaged trouble alarms; or severed communication, cable, or phone lines.

4.5 Storage and Distribution

There is a significant difference between outside providers who transport or handle your materials and those internal or external operations that store and distribute your materials. For the most part, the transportation and handling operations only hold or control the materials for short periods of time. For transportation providers, it can be a few hours to possibly a day or two. Storage and distribution providers may control your goods for days to months or even longer, depending upon your needs and agreements with them. This is why the security program needs to be customized specifically for the type of service provided by the storage and distribution operations.

The general security program that needs to be in place has traditional security measures, i.e., access controls, CCTV, alarms, etc. It is their application that will make the difference between general coverage and a tuned program with explicit and detailed requirements. The value and overall risk of the goods and material will dictate the intensity of the security program. However, there should always be a basic security plan and program for any storage and distribution service provider when your goods are in the care and custody of another. It also does not make any real difference whether the storage and distribution is an internal client or a company-owned process that does not use a 3pls (third-person logistics supplier) or other contracted provider. In fact, an in-house operation affords a closer relationship between your security program and the operation, since you are all within the same corporate or company umbrella. This company relationship adds an element of responsibility and accountability. Operations actions or inactions are more visible or transparent, since your access to them is direct and not hindered by B2B (business to business) gaps in time, distance, and communications.

4.5.1 Security Review of Facility and Location

As with other providers and handlers of your material, you must look into where the operations are located and what external security threats might exist. This also includes a review and inspection of any physical deficiencies that may cause vulnerability to the operation and your materials.

Crime statistics and general sociopolitical reviews are required to understand the current issues that local government contends with that might draw resources away from their general protection of your operation. Interviews with surrounding operations will elucidate current trends in the type and intensity of crimes against operations, transportation, and personnel. This must also include basic examination of the purveyors of the crimes committed in the area or region. Are they independents, primarily operating as opportunists? Are they organized? What is the scope of their organization? Are there local gangs or groups? Are they based on a national or cultural alliance? Are they syndicated? Answers to these questions will determine the scope of your security program. Do you only need to worry about the operation, or will you need to incorporate the entire environment encompassing your operation and material handling?

4.5.2 Transportation Security Review

Your material must be transported to and from your location. If you hold title to the material in or out of the facility, then you need to concern yourself with the security of the transportation of those goods. This is the case whether or not the transportation provider claims there are security measures in place. Security can be expensive, and it is prudent to examine the security of transportation providers handling goods in and out of storage and distribution centers. Providers will most likely regress to the mean with security. That is, they will do the minimum to either (a) attract business with claims of security (if that might be of interest to potential customers) or (b) provide only the minimum that is probably required of a local regulation and no more. Be circumspect in your examination and audit their plans to ensure that they provide the basics as advertised. Of course, if their measures are either lax or lacking, or inadequate for the security risks posed against your goods, then a detailed security plan must be developed. We will examine some of these risk and responses later, but for now, let your security review of the criminal environment of the area and region direct your focus on the level of detail required for a suitable security plan for the transportation provider.

4.5.2.1 Basics for Transportation   The basics of security for storage and distribution transportation providers are essentially the same as with regular transportation:

- All drivers properly vetted
  - Proper, valid, and current driver credentials and licenses
  - Drug screening prior to hiring
  - Criminal background check prior to hiring
  - Polygraphs of theft issues at hire
- Trucks and trailers fitted with highly secure locking devices
- Equipment in good operating condition

- Fuel capacity sufficient to either arrive at a destination without stopping or have enough range to move out of a high-risk locale or region
- Sufficient driver/base communications

The difference between a standard or minimal security program and an elevated and focused one can be that the transportation is moving goods of a known type and possibly great quantity. If your material involves storage and/or distribution of high-value/risk goods, then it is a simple deduction that transportation delivering or removing goods from your facility is carrying these goods in and out and nearly exclusively as FTLs (full truck loads). That is a lot of material, with the potential of a significant loss to you and your customers if stolen.

Remember to examine your agreement with the storage and distribution transportation provider(s). If a loss has a negative impact on your client or its customer(s), then your agreement with the transportation provider must include security details. In the event that another company holds title or liability to the goods prior to POD (proof of delivery) at your location, or when these are passed at handoff upon shipping out, then your security concerns can be more focused internally. When reviewing the agreement with providers, also involve your risk- and insurance-management folks to ensure that there are not any hidden or ancillary risks associated with a loss.

4.5.3 Shipping and Receiving

This is one of the most important security links in a storage and distribution supply chain security program. It is at these two points and functions that theft can occur and security gaps can be exploited with little or no detection. Good supply chain security management looks at these functions as part of the handoff element, and tight controls of security accountability, observation, and documentation is imperative.

Let's look at the potential gaps of receiving. The transportation provider arrives with your goods. There is a handoff to your operation and facility. Your normal receiving process is to ensure that all of the expected material arrives in good condition. Shortages and damages are to be documented in one form or another. The integration of security into your, or your vendor's, receiving program adds an additional perspective and layer of scrutiny. The manager or agent handler that is on your side of the handoff needs to consider and know what to look for in the event there has been a theft or pilferage or some other compromise of the material prior to its arrival at the facility.

The first step in this security scrutiny is having full documentation at the receiving facility of all information surrounding the arrival of the expected material prior to the arrival of the goods. This will include the mode of transportation and identifying information on that mode. Most likely it will arrive by truck, so we need to know the name of the firm, the license of the vehicle, the type of vehicle, and identifying information on the driver. The driver information must include the name and license number. A photo would be nice, too. A description and photo of the vehicle might be required. It will identify the vehicle upon arrival. And, there is another reason. If you have a security agreement with this provider, and elements of the agreement involve the actual driver and vehicle information, you will want to see that there is compliance to this security agreement. Some transportation agreements even go so far as to include mandatory vehicle identification schemes such as lettering on doors, sides, and roofs of the vehicle or trailer. All of this provides insight into any issues that might have developed on the road or with the transportation provider. Besides providing identifying information, this information is also important as to whom you are letting onto your property, who is handling your goods, and who will be held accountable in the event that issues are discovered.

As for the material you are expecting, you will be looking for the quantity and quality, of course. You will also be looking for information on the packing or packaging of this material. Is it loose? Is it wrapped with shrink-wrap? Possibly it is in cardboard or even wooden crates or containers. Are these containers strapped with plastic or steel bands? Are the bands and/or container lids sealed in some fashion? Are there serial numbers associated with those seals? What are the identifying numbers or codes? Obtain photos of the material and packaging if at all possible. These photos should be taken at the time of the loading onto the conveyance and not at origin unless it is on the conveyance that is expected at your operation. Origin photos are nice, as they provide an excellent visual of the material, but if there have been any handoffs prior to the transportation expected at your operation, it will not accurately represent the condition of the goods upon loading. Origin photos only provide the condition at the beginning of its trek, not after several handoffs and modes of transport. You will also be looking for the DIMs for the entire shipment and for each piece being handed off.

The next piece of introductory information you want is the date/ time of the expected delivery. Some operations limit the times and days of the week for deliveries and receiving, while others do not. In either case, it will be important to know when the material is expected. From an operations standpoint, this will enable the coordination of the necessary labor to receive the material. Looking through a security lens, this will add a red flag in the event the load is too late, or even too early. Any substantial change in travel and arrival time offers an opportunity to quiz the driver and the transportation provider of the reason for the time difference. Bizarre or out-of-the-ordinary explanations are possible tells of issues with the transportation and material, not to mention discrepancies between explanations by the operator and the provider or the provider's dispatch.

Having all of this preliminary information arms the security manager with the tools of observation and comparison. There are two main reasons for having these tools. One is that you will be able to detect issues with the material as it arrives, or even before it is off-loaded, thus offering opportunities to develop requisite security actions before the material is accepted and introduced into the inventory of the facility or operation. The other is that, depending upon how this material is later distributed or dispersed, issues of theft, pilferage, or other damages/compromises are not detected until way down the supply chain or when accepted by an end user. Your company might well be on the hook for these losses even though you provided a tight security program while the material was in your care and custody. If you unknowingly accept compromised material, you will also accept all liability and consequences.

Now that we have the prior notice and information out of the way, we move onto the actual delivery phase. When accepting delivery, you will also be afforded the opportunity to examine the load down to the piece level. This piece level will be down to whatever minimum configuration the material is in as shipped to you: loose cartons, wrapped cartons/boxes, skids, containers, crates—all pieces in one form or another. It is always a good idea to examine the contents of these pieces if possible. Creative thieves can bypass poorly wrapped or sealed packaging, thus hiding security issues. Even acceptable-looking containers could stand further examination, if at all possible.

All damages and discrepancies must be further investigated. This investigation must be immediate and the issue well documented. Plus, if at all possible, the entire shipment must be halted to enable a more detailed examination of all pieces in that shipment. Sometimes damages or discrepancies on the pieces are merely external representations of poor handling. There could be dents and tears caused by forklifts or close contact with transport containers or other material within the shipment. However, these, too, must be fully documented and investigated. External damage can be an indicator of internal damage. If, later in the supply chain, an end user reports internal damage, you may be able to associate it with your examination and documentation at the time of receipt from the transport.

For supply chain security purposes, external damage may be an indicator of a pilferage, theft, or even the introduction of unauthorized or dangerous material into a legitimate package or container. Certain government supply chain security programs (i.e., C-TPAT; see Chapter 8) require that any instances or suspected compromising of international or air cargo be fully investigated to detect and prevent the introduction and transportation of any material that, in and of itself or as a secondary element or article, could be used as a WMD (weapon of mass destruction). Further, drug interdiction laws also require full investigation to prohibit transportation and distribution of illegal drugs traveling within the legitimate supply chain.

Look at every issue, every piece. Small damages or rips and tears could have been an attempt to steal or to add to the material. They may also be a test to see whether or not the damage is detected and reported by your security program. It can be a test of how long it took to be noticed and how far down the chain it went before being noticed.

Small pilferages of items can also be tests to determine what kind of goods or materials are contained within the packaging. Often, there is little information on the external packing to indicate what kind of material is held within. A simple poke with a forklift blade or cut with a box knife will allow just enough room for a reach inside. Accidental cuts and tears happen, but none should be dismissed until investigated.

As we have said, small thefts might be an indicator of a test. These tests will tell the criminal about the type of contents and what external visual cues are on the packaging. If the material is targeted by criminals, they will now be able to see it coming from the outside and strike for larger quantities or even full loads.

Now that the entire delivery has been received, inspected, and introduced into your operation, the internal security measures you have in place will cover the material while in your care and custody, until you are ready to ship or distribute it.

Security of the shipping link in the supply chain is not a reverse mirror image of receiving. If you have a solid, integrated, and robust facility or operations security program in place, shipping of the material will be far less complex and far easier to facilitate. Since your receiving processes enabled you to fully recognize and document the condition of the material, then these conditions will still exist when preparing to distribute and hand off to the next link in the supply chain.

If you are handing off to a customer or end user and your responsibility will end with that handoff, then the security of the shipping portion of the relationship will further protect the material while in the last stages of care and custody. It will also exhibit your commitment to security to the customer because you took the appropriate and necessary security measures to care for what will soon be their material. From a customer service perspective, this will go a long way in your relationship with them and further help to build that relationship and customer loyalty for, hopefully, recurring business.

From an internal view, securing the material and goods while in your care and ensuring that they remain unmolested until handoff also protects your company or client from liability and other types of loss claims. Your detailed inspection and documentation upon receiving, coupled with internal security measures, "freezes" the condition of the material. With that said, this condition, well documented, provides proof that any issues farther down the chain, or after a customer receives it, did not occur with you or your client.

Security of the shipping phase begins with the selection of the material. Pick orders—or other methods of notification and determination of the material to be shipped—provide the identifying features of, data about, and descriptions of the goods. Selection from the inventory should be a straightforward process. However, since we know the condition of the material, we must be sure that that condition does not change from the point of being in inventory at the time of the pick or selection and the subsequent move to the shipping handoff. There should be a last-minute inspection of the material when being moved into the shipping area for preparation for release. The quickest way is a visual examination. Recommended is verification of all DIMs so that you can attest to the fact that it came out of inventory and was passed to the shipping process without change.

This is a good point to again put some emphasis on shrinkage. In the supply chain security world, shrinkage equals loss. Is there evaporation or some other environmental changes to the molecular composition of the material? If not, then what might have occurred in inventory that could have affected the weight or size of the goods? Also, was the receiving count and documentation correct? If you took in ten, did you really take in ten when now you only can find nine? Did someone misrepresent the count or DIMs? Or was someone able to circumvent your security program to pilfer or otherwise molest the material while in inventory? Verify the condition and DIM. Shrinkage is an indicator of a security breech.

Now that we can verify the condition and DIMs of the goods, we can develop accurate documentation and other shipping paperwork and information with confidence that we are shipping exactly what we say we are shipping.

The final phase of the security is to be sure that the transport fully reviews the material, examines its condition, and signs off on a clear POD. Once this is done, your security concerns over the material have been completed. If you are using vendors for receiving, storage and distribution, and then shipping, you will now need to move your focus to the transport and look ahead to the next handoff, wherever that may be. When using a vendor for storage/distribution, the security program for all the handling processes must either be in full compliance, or their internal security measures must fully cover what will be required for the protection of the goods. Audit their operation fully and often. Go there and observe, ask questions, and give direction. Do not leave it up to their security personnel. They look at their security program from the inside out, while you are viewing from the outside in, which gives a different perspective. Where the two meet should provide the optimal coverage. If theirs is lacking, then your program should take precedence over your material and goods.

4.6 Destination Concerns

If your supply chain security program has oversight all the way to destination, then there are some unique elements we should discuss. If, as in the previous section, your responsibility ends with a handoff at a point up the chain, then destination concerns have little or no bearing on your security program. However, if your program still retains responsibility for your client's material, then there a need for attention in this final stage. We will take this in two parts: (a) how it is received at destination by your operation and security and (b) how it is received by the operation of another.

Possibly, your material reaches destination and is then integrated into other uses, processes, or customers associated with your company or client. Or perhaps the material you have been protecting belongs to another, and destination is a point where they take it in for utilization. In these cases, there are some similar destination security requirements, and there are some that are dissimilar.

We will start with the similar ones. They are very close to or the same as the receiving security process, which was elucidated in the last section, especially if the destination phase is still within your purview. Simply put, it was received at destination in the same good condition that it was in at origin or, at the least, from the last handoff. Here now the material can be integrated in its expected condition and value. Whereas you may not have visibility into another's destination receiving processes, there should be similar processes in place that will replicate the quality of yours. It is always a good idea to coordinate with destination security management to review their security program: If it is lacking, then offer suggestions; if it is adequate, offer support.

The dissimilarity we will look at is how well the destination protects the material once the handoff is completed. If there is a clean POD and handoff, we can be fairly assured that all conditions were good; otherwise there would not have been a clean POD, etc. We should be asking "What if?" What if the destination's receiving security process is inadequate, insufficient, or poorly executed? What if there is a security gap that can be exploited and a situation exists where there could be a wide discrepancy of interpretations of the condition of the goods if issues are raised later? The IT world has a saying: GIGO (garbage in, garbage out). If security in the destination receiving process is poor, you could be embroiled in issues not of your doing.

The other dissimilarity is the protection of the material after a clean POD. And, for the purpose of this discussion, a clean POD is just that—nice and clean. This circumstance presents itself when the destination takes in the goods and then does little to protect the goods or material once placed in their inventory. Once they receive it, even though they signed off with a clean POD with no discrepancies or issues, their security program stops there. Often their operations take over, with little internal security oversight, with an assumption that if their material was taken in with a clean POD and their receiving process was good, then the material will forever be perfect, no matter how long or where it sits or is stored.

The reality is that, if no internal security measures are in place, the material or goods are open for theft, pilferage, and compromise. An example would be that goods under your care are delivered at a destination customer, and it is in good condition and signed off clean. The end user then takes in the material and places it on a rack or other storage location. They come back to the material days or even weeks later for use in their production and discover it opened, pieces missing, damage, or some other issue. This end user then comes back to you and claims that someone molested the material during your care and custody and that they, the end user, only discovered it now because it was hidden or missed at the handoff.

Remember handoff documentation? Receiving and shipping security and documentation? If you do and did those faithfully, you can rely on your program to show good care and handling. If you don't or you didn't, the end user might be able to make a case against your company or client. However, since you did and do have a tight supply chain security program, you can be confident when asking the end user how they secured the material after the handoff up to the point of their "discovery" of issues. You may hear several kinds of responses, ranging from their claims about their excellent security program, etc., to not hearing anything back from them about any alleged issues.

5

ELEMENTS OF A SUCCESSFUL SUPPLY CHAIN SECURITY PROGRAM

Development of a successful supply chain security program depends on a number of elements or ingredients. We have examined some pragmatic activities for use in the security program, and here we will look at some overarching elements that help to give the security program form and direction. Later we will look at more practical applications to help fit all the pieces together. The success of your program will rely on all those pieces, components, and applications working in unison.

5.1 Goal of the Supply Chain Security Program

The goal of an effective supply chain security program is really quite simple: Protect the goods, materials, and products from those who would take or hold them for their own. The supply chain security program should protect them from theft, pilferage, infiltration, and contamination while they travel end to end along the supply chain. The goal is simple, but the development and implementation of the methods and processes are not, as you are beginning to see. They are complex and detailed, and take an enormous amount of effort to develop, implement, monitor, and adjust.

This could also be stated in other contexts, based on what the focus or core competency might be for the company or client you represent. If you are in logistics, and your company is hired by customers to move materials and cargo along the supply chain, then you are looking to harden the materials entrusted to you against the onslaughts of criminal intent, thievery, and manipulation. If you represent the concerns of a risk management or insurance function, then you may be more intent to protect the goods, or ensure that they are protected by others, to limit liability of losses and theft, thus reducing claims, claims payments, and insurance premiums. Still others look at anti-terrorism, smuggling, or even piracy[1] as competing interests impacting the supply chain.

While we have looked at the supply chain in general and the vulnerabilities of those many links and ways to secure them, we also need to understand and examine more closely some of the conceptual contexts of the various internal topical interests when determining the methods we choose and, indeed, "why do we even care" in the first place. Supply chain security professionals, as in other professions and activities in business life, are sometimes looked upon to be *jacks-of-all-trades*. Still others are SMEs, or *subject-matter experts,* with very narrow or defined skill sets and knowledge. We will review some of these specialized security approaches to better illuminate why supply chain security has become so complex and multifaceted over the years. It is not our intent to become experts in these topics, but it is important to know that each approach has its own unique impact and motive that you must recognize to understand how it might influence your development of supply chain security plans.

5.2 Theft and Pilferage

Prevention of theft and pilferage might be viewed as the most basic of security goals. The criminal element is constantly looking for ways and means to commit cargo theft and to purloin goods out of the supply chain. It is safe to say that this has been an issue for as long as goods have been moved from point to point.[2]

If your assigned task is to protect against theft and pilferage, then that is your primary focus, and it should be the overarching goal of your security plan. You could be saying, "Well, sure, what else is new?" What is not new is that, when building a supply chain security plan, some designers lose their focus because they are too heavily influenced by other competing interests or pressures, and loss and theft prevention become ancillary instead of primary objectives of the program or plan. It is all about keeping your eye on the ball. You can be aware of your environment and surroundings, as well you should, but stay on course.

5.2.1 Smuggling and Contamination

Traditionally, smuggling activities are intent upon moving illicit goods past checkpoints that society has established to prevent those goods from being introduced into an area. This effort might be rooted in the fact that the goods are illegal to possess, such as narcotics, or it might be the result of government controls and prohibitions, as in embargoes between countries. Still others are looking to ensure that proper tariffs and taxes are levied and paid upon entry into regions or countries. Not to be overlooked is the atrocity of human trafficking. No matter what their particular nefarious interest might be, there are criminals who aim to get their particular "material" past the checkpoint or through the blockade.

The supply chain is affected when they attempt to use legitimate means for illegitimate purposes. Smuggling enterprises have always used their own methods of transportation and concealment. They fly their own planes over borders, tunnel under boundaries, and even pack submarines full for an underwater transborder excursion (see Figure 5.1). But it is their expertise in infiltrating your supply chain to conceal their own material—hiding behind the protective cover of your supply chain security program to evade detection—that should keep you awake at night.

This infiltration takes many forms. As we said, we are not trying to be interdiction experts, but you must be aware. You must be able to recognize the conditions that would facilitate these smuggling efforts. You can call in the experts for intervention and investigation, but if your security program is oblivious to smuggling methodology, your security program could be an unwitting accomplice to criminal activities.

Go back to our discussions about using DIM verifications (see Chapter 4) in an attempt to detect potential pilferage or weight-replacement thefts. This is also an excellent method to see if someone has added something to the material or to the containers used to transit the material or goods. Compromised airline ULDs (unit load devices) and other such transport containers are a common and effective concealment method (see Figure 5.2). If not for detecting the added weight, where there should not be any variance, a simple exterior examination could overlook this effort.

Figure 5.1   A narco-submarine (drug-smuggling sub) seized in Ecuador in July 2010. (*Source:* DEA press release. Courtesy Wikipedia Commons.)

There is an additional "why do I care" factor that may surface when considering your efforts to detect smuggling activities. Besides the illegal activities involved, there is *negative* brand recognition. The last thing your client or company wants to be known for is that they have been moving drugs, illegal materials, even people, without detection. Being caught up in these activities may also jeopardize your client's licensing, permits, and other governmental regulatory authorizations for moving, transporting, or distributing goods and products.

Figure 5.2   Compromised airline container.

We added *contamination* to this section, since some material moving in your supply chain could be, by its nature and composition, sensitive to environmental issues of air, temperature, or humidity. Further, the material might be sealed against the external introduction of foreign substances into formulated compounds, as in the case of many pharmaceuticals. If smugglers seek to conceal their material within these materials, there is a great risk that the product can be contaminated. In some instances involving FDA-regulated goods, a simple unauthorized manipulation or breaking of a container or a packing seal is enough evidence to require destruction of the material whether or not it was actually contaminated or altered. In other cases, some of these protected materials will have to be immediately returned to the place of manufacture for examination and recertification. That makes for a very unhappy customer and has direct impact on your revenue, since you will not be collecting for transportation or handling in either direction.

5.2.2 Antiterrorism

The antiterrorism elements added to supply chain security programs are twofold. The first is somewhat traditional. This involves terrorist organizations that obtain some of their funding from smuggling and the sale of illicit goods. Interrupting these goods interrupts the terrorist cash flow. The other is the attempt by terrorists to utilize the legitimate supply chain to conceal the movement of elements of mass destruction or other destructive materials and tactics. In September 2002, a container ship bound for the Port of Newark was detained outside New York Harbor for over two weeks because a preliminary examination of the ship's cargo suggested the presence of radioactive material. This initial detection and subsequent investigation ended with a benign result; however, it illustrates a potential method of concealment and a corresponding supply chain security response to that tactic. We are not advocating the scanning of all of your goods for radioactivity, but as it moves or is distributed, someone else might be examining the goods. Proper handoffs, inspections, and security applied to the goods will become critical evidence in the event of a positive scan or screening.

5.3 Government Supply Chain Security Program Compliance

It is imperative that you fully familiarize yourself with any and all government-sponsored supply chain security programs and regulations. Noncompliance with any number of these programs could result in fines, restrictions, censures, and even revoking of licenses, permits, and other types of accessibility to domestic and international logistics systems and businesses.

Depending upon company structure, these government compliance programs might be assigned to another function of the business other than security. They might be assigned to a "compliance" office, quality, even your legal office, since penalties could be harsh and the company might feel that the legal department should be called upon to defend the company against such actions.

No matter where these programs fall, you should be interacting with these functions as part of your education about the program and learning about the compliance plans your company is developing.

Some companies have placed compliance with these programs in other arenas, so you may find that the programs that are being developed or are already in place will duplicate many of the elements of a good internal supply chain security program. You may also find that the program you envision or are developing might be in conflict with what is perceived to be required to be in compliance with the government regulations and requirements.

Be careful of internal conflict when reviewing the compliance requirements with your counterparts in the other company BUs (business units). Some might see it as an infringement of their territory, or it might even spark a personal animosity toward the notion of being accused of inadequacy. These are social or interpersonal relationship issues, but failure to recognize them and the impact they could have on your program could very well block any attempts you make to build an effective security program. If some of the components of your plans require a compliance agreement or some type of support from other BUs or support functions, it would be wise to approach with an open mind. Try to understand what their focus is on their business—what are their responsibilities and even directives—and then see how these can be meshed with your own objectives. This may require negotiation skills to build a team or partnership relationship. It might even go as high up the food chain as having to educate the senior managers of the other functions as to why there should be an alliance and how it can benefit their BU's goals and objectives while also strengthening and protecting the organization against loss and criminality.

Another method to obtain their cooperation and collaboration is to find common ground and frame the issues not in terms of what will be beneficial for your supply chain security program, but what portions of your program will be beneficial to theirs. This is the traditional premise of making a sales pitch: Your target asks, "What is in this for me; how can I benefit?" Try to have this identified before you approach them with your concerns or ideas. Do not criticize or judge the validity or value of what they feel is important to them. It very well may be that it comes from a directive or that they have some other ownership associated with the content of their program(s).

In any case, look to see what plans and programs others in your organization might be implementing in response to these government supply chain security and compliance programs. You may be able to enhance theirs, borrow from them, or align with them. No matter how it is achieved, there will be compliance that will satisfy the government requirements coming from your supply chain security program and/or other internal compliance programs.

5.4 Customer Contractual Obligations

Contracts and agreements with customers on how you and/or your providers will handle, transport, and distribute their material could drive much of your supply chain security program. For example, if you are a ground transportation company that primarily handles material of little or no "criminal interest," I am sure that your security program may be limited to only driver checks and DOT (Department of Transportation) or other motor vehicle compliance regulations. However, simply add to the situation that the load you are carrying today is an FTL (full truck load) of microchips or possibly consumer electronics, and now your program is woefully insufficient. In the absence of a security directive, mandate, or requirement from the owner of these goods, an attentive supply chain security professional will recognize the risk and develop a correspondingly robust security plan as a responsibility to protect these goods while in the care and custody of your client or company.

Experience shows that owners and manufacturers of high-risk and high-value goods of any type have become well aware of the risk to their goods while in transit or while in off-site storage facilities. These entities have recognized the need to develop their own supply chain security programs. These are designed for their particular product or material and may be adjusted to fit the different transport, storage, and even socioeconomic and geographical environments that will surround their goods until they reach the end users.

The customer, in these cases, then pushes down their supply chain security program to your organization to seek compliance. These security requirements are a priority with the customer and they will expect it to be yours, also. Appendix A is an example of customer-generated security. It will not concern them that their material may only be a portion of all the goods and materials your company might handle. They will demand compliance with their security program no matter the cost or effort required. You will need to impress upon your client or company the criticality of the customer's supply chain security program and any costs and other company resources it might consume for fulfillment. This cannot be a simple matter of agreeing to the security program in order to obtain the business, or of agreeing to the requirements with the thought that they are mostly likely not needed or are easily implemented.

In some instances, a customer might confirm or eliminate a potential supplier or vendor for their service based on their opinion of the vendor's ability to comply and maintain their security program. In other situations, there could be insurance and other risk-management considerations. If you are found to be out of compliance, you run the risk of losing the business. You also might be violating a clause in the agreement and be required to pay out higher claims, fees, or premiums than originally negotiated or considered.

Going back to the adage that security can contribute to a company by either making money or saving money, proper management of a customer security program can do both. It may help to win the business. And by identifying security costs, the contract negotiators will have that information available to bargain with the customer to pass through, share, and absorb any combination of these costs that could impact the revenue associated with this contract.

This is another example of the importance of ensuring that any supply chain security program that would exist for your customer's goods be reduced to writing and incorporated in the agreement or contract between your company and its customer.

5.5 Risk Management

You will also perform this task to protect your company or client from claims of loss or theft. Considering that they are the ones who are signing your paycheck, you might want to also view security programs for yourself and for customers through a "protective" lens. In some instances, agreeing to a customer's supply chain security program without a proper review and analysis of your capabilities can place your company in a precarious position of extensive liability and exposure to monetary losses in the event of a theft or some other violation or breach of a customer's security program.

You should not negotiate an agreement or contract without closely scrutinizing the security efforts required. In like manner, look to verify that your client's or company's risk managers have also reviewed the documents. If they have not, then you should be notifying them and require that they perform their own risk-management analysis. There may already be insurance clauses within the agreement. What is important to you is that, in the event of a failure that might be linked to or interpreted as a security failure, you can identify how your company will be exposed to monetary compensation back to the customer. Remember that many claims-loss payments can directly impact the bottom line of your client. Shareholders will be keen to notice if there have been payouts due to losses where there might have been an opportunity to provide some insulation against the loss based on adroit contract language. There might be additional language about damage, service failures, and other nonsecurity-related exposure that is not within your realm. However, you would be surprised to see the lack of security review of customer contracts where simple liability language exists within the agreement, or in a security clause or section, but where more restrictive language exists within another section unrelated to your security program. Read the entire agreement or contract. Read it with one eye looking to identify security concerns and with the other eye tilted toward risk management and protecting that paycheck.

5.6 Industry Positioning and Branding

The saying goes something like this: "Do a good thing for somebody, and they will tell three people. Do something bad, and they will tell seven." The brand of a company is as valuable as its assets. The position the company occupies within its own industry is equally important. The higher or more pronounced the positioning, and the more distinct the brand recognition, the better it is for the company. Brand positioning refers to "target consumers" who see a reason to buy your brand in preference to others. It ensures that all brand activity has a common aim: that it be guided, directed, and delivered by the brand's benefits/reasons to buy; and that it focus on the consumer at all points of contact.[3]

Branding, besides the projected icons and other representations of trade names, trademarks, insignias, etc., usually rests within the functions of the company's corporate communications, sales, and marketing groups. There is an additional component of branding, and that is the *image* of the company. Are they fair and honest in dealing with customers? Are they sensitive to the environment? Are they compliant with the rules and regulations of their industry? The image characteristic of the company brand is where your security program will be of the greatest influence. Some companies go to great lengths to ensure that internal wrongdoings never reach the general public. It is called *negative attention*, and no one needs it.

A well-developed, well-implemented, and well-managed supply chain security program will enhance the image of your company. Repeated or several large failures in your security program may hurt more than not. As you have seen, some companies of any industry might carry a reputation—some for the quality of their goods, the cost of their goods, style, design, or any number of attributes. The same is true for your client or company. Depending upon what industry you are in or function within, transportation, handling, storage, distribution, etc., someone out there has an opinion about it at some level. Hopefully it is positive. So should be your security program. Supply chain security is an industry within an industry. Supply chain security is a specialized function. It requires expertise with a unique way of looking at the service of security. Your expertise in supply chain security programs is demonstrated within the industry where your client operates. Since much of your program will impact the materials and/or functions of others, your program, as well as your company, will develop a reputation surrounding security.

This reputation may have a profound impact on the positioning of your company within its particular industry. Companies look to position themselves as the most prominent, the most reliable, and the most capable providers within their industry. You can help or hinder that position. You must keep this in mind at all times as you implement your security program. It is also vitally important when dealing with the customer. Everything you do, say, and exhibit will reflect on your ability to run a successful supply chain security program. This attribute will also reflect on your client or company. Rarely is a company's security program beyond the sight of its customers. Even fully internal programs that deal only with their own materials, providers, handlers, etc., and that are not shared with any outside supplier or customer help to fashion an internal security culture. This culture provides a small particle or element of the overall corporate culture. Unless your company operates in a vacuum, someone from the outside world will come in contact with your company and experience, even slightly, how the company operates, supported by an internal corporate culture.

Another aspect of how the rest of the industry will view your company and how it might impact the company's industry position and its supply chain security program is how it handles crisis. If there is an event that negatively impacts a customer's material and it involves a security incident, the approach of the security portion of the event will demonstrate as much about your program as any other positive attributes it possesses or can provide. A prompt, aggressive, and appropriate response to an incident is critical. This is not only from an investigative aspect, but also from a service perspective toward the customer. (This also applies to internal stakeholders, as they also need to see an appropriate security response.) If a customer detects a slow or unresponsive attitude, there is a significant chance that your company will come under fire in general, as well as your security program specifically. This is to be avoided at all costs. While it may be difficult to quantify any damage to the customer–company relationship, you can be assured that it will cause consternation in the short term, and if it is not resolved or if similar occurrences are repeated, your company's brand will be negatively affected.

5.7 Marketing and Sales

Marketing and sales (M&S) operates on a platform of expectation. They sell a service or product to customers, and the customers have an expectation of what they will be receiving. This expectation might be based on a time frame, the quality of a product, ROI (return on investment), or any number of values the customer has placed on the items or services transacted. Some research has shown that ratings satisfaction is directly related to customer expectation and, as well, that negative customer experiences are more intense than positive ones.[4] If an expectation of the quality of a product is high and that expectation is achieved, then a high degree of satisfaction is also achieved. You may say that this seems to be common sense. However, interestingly, if there is a low expectation of a service, and that low expectation is also produced, there is not a great loss of satisfaction. If you do not expect much, and you do not get much, you feel that you have received what you expected. If you expect greatness and you do not receive it, then your expectations were not met, and satisfaction suffers. If your expectations are low, but you receive a higher than expected quality, then your satisfaction level is vastly improved.

Why the M&S lesson? It is because your company operates on revenue received from the successful sale and marketing of its services or materials. And, if your supply chain security program impacts the ability of your company to provide quality services or materials, then you need to know about how your client's M&S group works: how they approach potential customers, what these potential customers are being offered by your organization, and what is it that they expect to receive from your company. If security is an element of that service or product and the customer has an expectation of a certain level of security, then your program needs to reflect that expectation, and perform at or above that level.[5] Failure to acknowledge this element—and the influence it could play—would seriously hinder or negatively impact the customer relationship and future customer loyalty, and that all spells lost revenue for your company.

References

1. "Pirates' hideouts and knowledge of trade routes allowed them to attack many cargo ships. Because cargo ships were unexpectedly being taken over, goods were not arriving in appropriate ports on time. Many people in those ports depended on this cargo for income. Piracy hurt people's livelihoods and the colonies' economies. The English government and the American colonial governments had to figure out what they could do to stop piracy and keep the colonies and trade routes from further problems. The government began posting rewards for the capture and/or killing of pirates and also allowed private ships to attack pirate ships. Often, when a pirate was killed, his body was hung at the opening of a harbor to remind pirates of what could happen to them. Because the government wanted to rid the seas of piracy completely, pardons were sometimes awarded to pirates so they could come forward, stop their lives of crime, and not get in trouble. This was rare, however. Because of the efforts of the English government and American colonies, piracy along the Atlantic trade routes slowly diminished." Amy Johnson, "Pirates and Economics," History Essays, Week 3—October 25, 1999. http://www.sitesalive.com/hl/99f/private/essay/hle991025.htm.
2. "Cargo theft is an ancient profession in this part of the world. Afghanistan was once part of the Silk Road (the trade route between the Middle East and China). The caravans had to pay a lot of attention to security. In Afghanistan, stealing from these caravans was considered great and lucrative, if a very dangerous, sport. Some things never change." *Pounding Sand,* Strategy Page. http://www.strategypage.com/htmw/htlog/articles/20120124.aspx.
3. "Brand Positioning; Definition and Concept," *Management Study Guide,* 2011. www.managementstudyguide.com.
4. Richard L. Oliver, *Satisfaction: A Behavioral Perspective on the Consumer* (New York: M.E. Sharp Inc., 2010).
5. Osmond Vitez, "Why Is the Expectation of a Consumer Important in Marketing?" *Demand Media,* 2012, www.smallbusiness.chron.com/expectation-consumer-important-marketing-789.html.

6

Methodology for Supply Chain Security

Methodology in the scientific sense is "a system of broad principles or rules from which specific methods or procedures may be derived to interpret or solve different problems within the scope of a particular discipline. Unlike an algorithm, a methodology is not a formula but a set of practices."[1]

In the supply chain security world, methodology is our style, our manner, our processes, and our *practices* of how we integrate or interject security into the very fabric of the business or organization. Security must be assimilated into the culture of the company. It must be as much of the day-to-day routine as doing e-mails, writing reports, and performing our daily assignments and tasks. How we get there is more like blending an amalgam than being an overseer or providing a protective shell. These are also viable security methods, but if security is to be truly integrated in the organization, it must occupy a place in the operational mindset of every employee at all levels of the business. It also involves our providers and vendors, but we cannot get there from here until our own house is in order. Only then can you expend the energy into converting others to your way of thinking about the applications of your supply chain security program.

6.1 Integration into the Business

It is often a hard row to hoe when you are trying to get the requisite attention and acknowledgment from senior management for a true integration of security into the organization. Some perceptions of security have it as a guard at the door, keeping the fox out of the henhouse. Or possibly it is more closely associated with policing, with enforcement of rules and regulations. Approaching management with your expectation of being a peer, in the political sense, with other organizational functions can be a reach for some leadership. Your goal will be to sell your program to each and every functional unit. The message and content will definitely need to be adjusted to the unit you approach.

It is much like knowing your audience when preparing for a speech or lecture. To be an effective speaker, you need to know 110% of the content as well as the current level of understanding of the topic by your audience. Knowledge of the demographics of the people would also help, as well as their general level of knowledge of the organization.[2]

If you take the time to prepare your material and the approach to your audience, your program is far more likely to be understood, and the value of your program will also be appreciated. With some groups, you will look to impart a lot of information, with others not so much. In any case, do not leave any group out of your program. If nothing else, members of these units would be the ones in the field who see the company processes and operations every day and could alert you to a potential security issue long before it develops into a disaster. Ideally, you are looking for *your* security program to become *their* security program. You want it to be in their mind-set as it is in yours. In effect, you want assimilation, not only integration.

6.2 Business Unit Support

Here is the "buy-in" we need from all of our business units. Your security program needs their support for it to be more accepted, more universally practiced, and more blended into the operational culture. Your mission is to sell them not only that you need their support and assistance, but that they need yours, too. This will be the situation where you will need to answer the questions of "What's in it for me?" or "How can this be of value to me or my group?" As mentioned previously, you must know your audience. Know what they do and know what is important to them. When you are selling, be sure to clarify what it is they need from security. If they are not sure, then dig deeper to find out what their group might need or, in the case where customers are involved, try to determine what they think or what *the voice of the customer* might be saying about security. For sales, you can support their customers who are sensitive to loss from either a monetary or productivity point of view. If risk management is the issue, then you might emphasize a reduction of claims, a drop in insurance premiums, etc. From an operational perspective, the relevant focus could be a reduction in transportation or handling-time issues due to interruptions that might be caused by security failures or other related matters.

The methodology here is demonstrating, exhibiting, or explaining the practices, procedures, protocols, and values of your security program that are, or could be, tailored and customized for a particular business unit (BU) or group for their benefit. If you can accomplish this, then you will also benefit—as well as the company as a whole.

6.3 Structure and Reporting

We will divert from discussing outward practices of methodology at this point to examine an important internal component of an effective supply chain security program. I mention this here because a well-developed and -constructed security structure is better able to deliver its programs and practices than one that is disorganized or incongruent with the organization it is attempting to service. The structure of your security organization should augment or enhance the operational ability of the client. While it needs to function well, it should be designed to facilitate the business and not be segregated from the goals of the company. Here is an example. Say that you have a practice in your security program that calls for all visitors and employees to be subject to a search of their person upon leaving a high-security pick-and-pack operation. But the pick-and-pack facility is unaware of this rule, since the field security manager you have is relegated to providing traditional corporate-office security instead of being assigned to the priority of potential loss and theft at a high-value pick-and-pack. Another would be that the security personnel are more aligned with business units who have little to do with the operation needing security presence and intervention, like warehousing, distribution, or transportation.

Align your organization to facilitate the business—to help the organization to function without interruption or experiences of loss.

If there are field operations, then your focus should be in the field; if the vulnerability is more central to a specific operation or function, then there is your emphasis.

Another important consideration is hierarchy. The most effective security programs I have seen have been closely associated with or under the management direction of either operations or risk management. Operations likes security because it helps keep the facilities, the people, and the material secure. Risk management likes it because integration of security will enable a reduction of loss, theft, and subsequent claims. Security overseen by management, such as human resources and even the legal department, are too far removed from the day-to-day understanding and connectivity needed in the field of security and the security requirements needed within the various operational and business units.

While having a flat organization can facilitate communication, feedback and decision making to management in a quality supply chain security organization still need a clear line of reporting. If you are fortunate enough to have personnel assigned to your program on a dedicated basis, then you can have a specific and committed reporting structure. They report to you; you to a senior member of the company; and so on. In many cases, due to cost-containment and operational priorities, security management is a shared task along with another operational or other business function. In these instances, the business or functional side usually has priority. It is not unusual for a warehouse manager to also be the site security manager, or for the health-and-safety office to also have security in its title. Here they will provide those priority services and have a direct reporting line to their BU management. They would also have a lesser, "dotted line" reporting to your program. This can be a challenge, especially if there is a large security issue to handle or if the security program needs more attention that the operational unit management can spare.

This does not mean that the reporting will be weak or disconnected. It may only mean that you might have to wait your turn or be willing to explain and ask for consideration from the other BU manager in order to complete your tasks. In these cases, you should ensure that this shared reporting is clearly understood by both the management and the personnel assigned. This will provide them with guidelines for accomplishing security goals and also highlight the security-reporting priorities.

6.4 Responsibilities and Roles

The responsibilities and roles of security are often closely aligned with the reporting structure of your security function. However, while one tends to be an administrative piece, the other is more practical in its ability to deliver security to the supply chain. In other words, *role* is where you are, where you fit in, what part you play in the big picture of the goals and strategies of the organization within the structure, and what level of influence you may have over others. *Responsibility* is what is expected of you within that role. Your role might be dependent upon the reporting structure; or rather, the reporting structure has several roles or levels to populate, and with it comes what each of these roles requires from you and how you will communicate those functions.

It is these responsibilities and roles that enable the policies, protocols, and practices of your supply chain security program to be communicated, implemented, and monitored. These myriad tasks are undertaken by those in these roles, fulfilling their responsibilities and communicating through the reporting structure.

With that said, it is important that there be a clear understanding of what the role and responsibility of the person in that position might be. Ambiguity blurs boundaries, in this case roles and responsibilities. If the security manager is not clear on what is expected or what boundaries are in place, two things might happen. The first is to withdraw from active decision making for fear of "overstepping my bounds" or the opposite. Boundaries are often crossed when it is unclear where they exist. These unplanned and possibly unwelcome transgressions could be interpreted as impinging on another's role or responsibility, creating unnecessary conflict.

The effect on your supply chain security program can as well be negatively affected. If a security program is viewed as overly aggressive or zealous (even if it is only a perception), then others in the organization could become reticent when interacting with your program. The resultant breakdown in communications could seriously set back your program.

When developing the roles and responsibilities of your managers, there might be some tasks that are not strictly security related. There could be some that are closer to a quality- or risk-management function. As long as these tasks do not conflict with security, but rather are complementary, then it is perfectly acceptable to include them. However, it must be a clear and concise responsibility, so as not to bleed over into another organizational function.

6.5 Policies and Procedures

Policies and procedures (P&Ps) are the backbone of your supply chain security program. They provide direction and explanation of the security you provide for the organization. The P&Ps give a clear understanding of what it is that you are providing, where it is to be applied, and how it is intended to impact the organization. They offer a guide, or roadmap, to how the function of supply chain security interacts, blends, and weaves itself into the overall activities, tasks, goals, and objectives of the company. They also illustrate to others in the company what may be expected of them. This is extremely important. Using a principle from Pareto's Rule of 80/20,[3] I see that the security policies and procedures are either acted upon or enforced by 80% of the organization. The remaining 20% is under the scrutiny and circumspection of your security organization. This means that you rely heavily on others to follow through on the security you have developed. If you want their cooperation and dedicated effort, then they must have a clear understanding of what it is that is expected of them. They also need to know why. As discussed previously (see Chapter 5), for a person to fully embrace a concept for which they may be held responsible, they need to be able to relate or identify with that concept. They need to know why it is important to them, and in the case of supply chain security, why it is important to the organization.[4]

If they understand the purpose of the procedure as well at its application, they will be more likely to accept the responsibility of enforcing or properly applying the technique. Appendix B provides an example of the form/format for effective policy publication.

There are several mandatory elements in the development and subsequent implementation of your supply chain security policies and procedures. The first is to know the difference between the two. The *policy* is the overarching reasoning behind or the focus of the actions you wish to have in place. It should set the objective, even the philosophy, of the guiding principle. The *procedure* is the action needed to implement or sustain the policy. The procedure is a detailed description of the steps or actions needed to effect a change or maintain a condition.

The next is to have the P&Ps fully accepted by senior management. If they do not understand and support the P&Ps you have developed, the program will fail. The organization's population will not follow, and you will not have the support of management to enforce compliance by others. In fact, when issuing policies and procedures, there should be a reference within or attached to the policies stating that they come with the full support and authority of senior management. This way, there is no mistaking that they are to be viewed as a "company" security policy and not simply a BU-level policy or guideline.

The next step is the rollout and training. Obviously, the rollout is the announcement or publication of the P&Ps. Some companies like to make these corporate-wide announcements with some level of fanfare. Others are subtler in their communication culture. In any event, the targeted audience of the P&Ps must be fully and officially informed. After the rollout comes the training or acclimation phase. The people who will be responsible for carrying out the procedures must understand how they work and the roles they will play in implementing the procedures. The more complicated the procedures, the more intense and detailed the training must be. This training takes many forms, from simple instructions attached to the procedures, to actual classroom-type instruction, testing, and validation or certification. Never assume that the population can put the procedures into operation without training. The fact that you have introduced these policies and procedures to enhance the security of your company means that there is a new or modified method of operation. Whenever there is a change in the norm, the affected groups need to understand, accept, and then practice the procedures to be effective and compliant. If the P&Ps are more radical or if they are replacing a long-term program, then it would be wise to apply change-management techniques to your program and its delivery to the group. According to the Aveta

Business Institute, one effective change-management technique is to "label any type of change as a 'transition.' If your company is going through a business change right now then it calls for a professional change for you. Now, one way for you to manage this kind of change is to think that you are in the space between two things. This is a transition and through this, you will be able to create a better [security] future."[5]

A consideration in implementing a P&P that will be expected to be in place over a long period of time is the condition of *social norming*. This is the condition within a company or organization that impacts the level of practical application of a rule, policy, procedure, etc. Sociologists generally define social norming as "rules developed by a group of people that specify how people must, should, may, should not, and must not behave in various situations."[6]

It lies under the surface and is representative of the informal communication network that exists within all organizations. It is important to understand this as you implement your policies and procedures. Once your ideal policy and set of procedures are in place and the targeted audience has been trained and set to task, you cannot assume that they will follow these procedures and policies forever and always. As with other directives, people need reinforcement and guidance to maintain the expected level of competency. They will forget a step, cut a corner, or even ignore segments of the program for a variety of reasons. Some are due to time limitations, difficulty of the tasks, lack of ability, or possibly social norming.[7] The operators begin to realize that other people are not following the procedures, and they receive subtle peer pressure to (a) conform with the noncompliant behavior of the others or (b) regress their effort to a midpoint where they are not really out of compliance, but are not really following the program as it was designed or required.

To counteract these defeating measures, you must be sure to monitor the effectiveness of your program. Review and audit it on a regular basis to ensure compliance. In some cases, you may need to perform some retraining or adjusting of the procedures for inconsistencies or misaligned outcomes that revealed themselves with practical application.

6.6 Training

We touched briefly on training in the previous section as it related to implementation of policies and procedures. However, training has a broader application for the furtherance of your supply chain security program.

For your security programs to be truly effective and integrated into your company's or client's business, it must be fully communicated, understood, and practiced by every person in the organization. Each person might have a different perspective, exposure, or responsibility as it comes to security; however, each in their own way must practice security for their function, role, and situation in the operation of the company. To accomplish this, the security program must be presented to them, explained to them, and then applied by them. This involves training at all levels, from the most senior to the very basic worker. Senior management might not need training in the practical applications of your supply chain security program, but they need some exposure to see what it is that you are trying to develop and implement and to understand how it positively impacts the company. Mid-level managers need yet another level of understanding, since they need to advance the program and recognize how they may be required to implement it and supervise its application and monitor the employees or workers in the fulfillment of the program. Workers should be trained on how the security program affects the company and its operation as well as themselves, and how they will be required to follow the procedures or guidelines.

Training should be given across the board, system wide, at all levels and at all locations. Universal application of security is essential if it is to be integrated into the culture of the operation. Besides your supply chain security program's goal of protecting your company's, client's, or customer's assets, materials, or goods, it goes a step further. A well-implanted security program adds a sense of well-being to the environment of the organization. We mentioned how security can be marketed to customers or clients to exhibit how you would care for their materials. Security within the organization also sells the population on the point of caring. Policies and procedures of access control, personnel identification, visitor control, perimeter control, search policies, etc., also radiate a sense of protection to those who work in and belong to the organization. Many standard security applications, such as CCTV coverage, have a dual effect. One is an obvious application of monitoring the conditions of the safeguarded materials and their handling. Yet, it also adds to a calming and positive psychological effect of the feeling that someone is watching over them, offering some level of protection. An example would be the presence of external building or facility CCTV coverage. It watches the building, but it also watches parking lots, stairways, and other areas where employees enter, exit, park, work, or take breaks. It is not unusual for human resources to request coverage of employee parking areas. It adds to the sense of protection for the security and safety of the employee while on company property.

This sense of well-being comes from an understanding that security is an integral part of the operation and that it is applied at all levels. This feeling of safety, from an individual perspective, is reinforced when the employees have been properly informed and received training in the organization's security program.

6.7 Classifications

Classifications take into account different levels or risk and vulnerability that might exist from location to location, from function to function, or from provider to provider. When a security program is developed, it generally has universal application. In other words, an element of a security program can be applied to just about any operation anywhere.

Not all organizations need the same level of security, and in many cases, not all locations or operations of an organization need the same level of security. The level of risk should dictate the appropriate level of the security response based on the threat, the value of the material, the actual handling, or the functions involved surrounding the material. As you develop or seek to implement a security program, you should also take into account the practicality of that security program. You should evaluate the necessity for any given security application. One method of doing this is to have a classification process.

Classification looks at the operation as levels. One part of the operation might have more risk, others less. One location might be more vulnerable than others. It would not be practical or efficient to universally apply a security policy to locations that have no need or requirement for that particular security process. Your security program will, no doubt, have many elements that are useful and essential throughout the operation, at all locations. However, mandating a security application that is not needed or impractical is a waste of effort, time, and expense. It also could undermine your general program when others inside your organization view these inefficiencies and incongruent applications. Seeing this lack of fit could lead to a lack of confidence that your program is considerate of the business needs of the organization or its customers.

Classifications can be developed by examining the organization and understanding the security risks, threats, and vulnerabilities of the operation. Some of the considerations are geographic location, value of the material, storage and handling requirements, or transportation methods and requirements. Once these are determined, you can take these elements and overlay them onto each operation or location of the business. As with the alignment of a stencil, you can begin to see which elements are the same, which are different, and which might not be required. Most likely, many will have widespread use and applicability. However, you will see where a security procedure, program, or element is not supportive of that location or, in an opposite direction, where it is not sufficient to mitigate a security risk, threat, or vulnerability. The result is likely to be that where one location has a high level of security, the level of security needed at another location is somewhat less.

The more there are different functions that are not shared by all locations, the more you will see the need for classification. Plus the more, or less, the value of the materials, goods, or services from place to place, the more (or less) security is required to protect these products.

Classification should categorize levels from high to low: A, B, or C; high, medium, or low; red, yellow, or green; or whatever is more easily understood for your operation. No matter the label, the intent is to understand the security need and apply the appropriate response and program. An example of the usefulness of classifying a location or operation would be the security program for the installation and use of a high-value cage. Generally, high-value cages are used to isolate and control the access to high-value or high-risk materials or goods from the general work force. They are kept under strict control with CCTV and other documentation procedures, with limited and controlled access by select people. The cages are mostly of durable-gauge steel or metal-wire-mesh sides, extended to the ceiling or topped with wire roofs, covered by CCTV from various angles, having controlled access at doorways or gates, and alarmed in some manner.

Having a high-value cage (HVC) (see Figure 6.1) of this type is certainly appropriate from a location handling, storing, or distributing high-value goods and materials. High security = Level A = high level of intensity for security applications = high-value cage. At another location for the same company, we can imagine that the most valued product or material could be magazines meant for distribution. In this case, it would be unwise to mandate that your company or client or service provider should have an HVC installed and in use at all their locations. Low security = Level B = less intensity of security application = maybe just a fence or marked designated area under CCTV coverage for general documentation of conditions.

Figure 6.1   High-value cage.

As operations change, so should the classification. As customers, materials, clients, etc., change, so should the classification. It is good practice to review and potentially reclassify a location or operation yearly. This way, you will be able to assess any changes in security, up or down, that might be required. If a location or operation has a high rate of turnover of these variables, you may wish to reclassify biyearly or quarterly.

Once you have developed the content of your classification evaluation and structure, you will be better able to assess the actual security needs of that specific location. In the next section, we will discuss security reviews and assessments. These processes are linked to classifications in that they, too, are adjusted to properly measure the actual security requirements of a site or location. You will see that the classification offers the foundation of the security assessment to accurately audit and determine how well that location is applying and following your customized security plan based on the classification of that operation.

6.8 Security Auditing and Assessments

Now that you have classified a location or operation based on the level of security risk and have formulated a customized security plan for that location based on the level of security response required to mitigate those risks, you will need to establish a method of assessing the level or state of compliance of the implementation of those programs, processes, and procedures. Appendix C is a very basic example, but it gives you an idea of the many security issues that should be covered, reviewed, and assessed.

Auditing is the way you determine whether your supply chain security program is being followed. It first tells you that the particular element of the security required at the operation or location has been implemented and exists. Then it tells you at what level it is being followed. The results offer insight into how well the programs are being followed and what security gaps exist within the operation. Gaps in your security program offer a vulnerability opportunity for things to go wrong, which is why you have a supply chain security program in the first place. The audit reveals the gaps and presents an opportunity for you to set corrective action plans (CAPs) into motion to close those gaps as quickly as possible.

The determination of the state of compliance to your security plan can generally take two forms. One is the audit, and the other is a review or survey. The difference between the two is the way in which you rate the state of affairs. The audit should be developed with a more quantitative result, while the survey is more of a qualitative study. Each has its own merits.

First we will look at the audit. We take a lesson from our friends across the hall in accounting. In the financial world, audits are used to determine if any one set standard is being followed or not. It examines what is required or mandated to be in place; then it judges whether or not that process is being followed or not. It offers a range of measurements, and it verifies computations, tallies, and results. Most common outcomes of financial audits are authentications of the financial results and how those were obtained. These are detailed and specific. They also offer a view of how the results match financial expectations or requirements. Generally accepted accounting principles (GAAP) serve as the plan for companies as they develop their economic programs and balance their books. Financial audit seeks to determine whether the operators of the company have deviated from GAAP. That deviation points to potential errors and, in some cases, misconduct. Some financial audits also offer a rating of compliance to GAAP and other accounting measures. The ratings are offered as a number like a debit ratio or a sliding scale from 1 to 10, with compliance being 10. There are also health ratios; or the rating could be as simple as a red/yellow/green classification to determine whether a process is being followed or not: red for noncompliance, yellow for partial, and green for full compliance. Each level carries its own escalation process to achieve compliance.

In the world of supply chain security, this auditing method is quite useful. A specific security process is examined to measure if it is being followed or not. The end result is a specific measurement for that process. That result would be combined with the results and measurements from the examination of all the other security processes of the program. This end result would give another rating that offers a determination on the level of compliance for the entire operation. On a micro level, it can pinpoint a security gap in a process. On a macro level, it gives you a view of the overall "health" of your supply chain security program. Be it 1 to 10, high to low, red to green, you can assess the situation, measure the level or risk, and use this information to determine the level of response required to close the gaps and protect the operation.

One thing that an audit-based assessment does not do is to consider mitigating circumstances. The audit is more black and white. Is the plan being followed or not? Is the process or procedure in place or not? It will pick up a partial compliance, but it does not modify the result based on a subjective response or condition.

Security reviews or surveys take a different tack in the examination and determination of security compliance. While it is still important to measure if the process is in place and to determine the level of compliance to the rules, it allows for other circumstances to affect how compliance might be reached or accomplished, or why full compliance does not exist, or whether partial compliance presents a security gap or risk to the operation. Noncompliance due to error or malfeasance is still easily revealed and measured, having little or no mitigating circumstances to explain the deficiencies. However, the security survey method measures if the security process is in place and the level of compliance, and then takes into account (a) what operational conditions exist that cause a less-than-full-compliance result or (b) that the intent of security procedure was obtained, but by an approach other than expected or directed. The end result is that you see the compliance and you also see how that compliance was obtained. The micro result shows the level of compliance; the macro result still gives you an overall report or condition of your supply chain security program. However, the value in the security review is twofold. One is that it offers a more flexible view of the program and its effectiveness; the other is that it elucidates potential advantages of how to obtain the same result, but in a different way. Possibly the other way can be cost effective or less complex, which would enhance its position within the organization. It also reveals ways in which a security policy or procedure might be circumvented without detection. This could call for a redesign of a security policy or procedure.

There is another difference between security audits and reviews, which both relate to subjectivity. The audit will determine a rating.

That rating will fall somewhere between full and poor or noncompliance—the pass/fail condition. The results of a security review offer the detection of security gaps, which are then analyzed for their criticality and the development of CAPs. You might choose to utilize either the audit or survey based on to whom the results are passed and reviewed. Internally, audits are received as a formal status report that calls for corrective action to be implemented and completed over a specified period of time.

However, if the audience of a security report is a customer or other noninternal recipient, you may wish to use the review style. It appears as a less rigid, cut-and-dried report. With a pass/fail or numerical determination, the recipient might view the security program as failing and be apprehensive of continuing the relationship based on a fear of loss, pilferage, or theft. Even detailed explanations have a difficult time in clarifying the security conditions.

The survey, on the other hand can be offered as a self-policing tool to the client or customer. It shows that you are looking into your program for gaps and that you correct those gaps when they are found. Even with a number of gaps reported, it can give you leeway into how the audit is perceived. Another way of looking at it would be to offer the results of a security audit to a client for a warehouse distribution location as a "fail." The customer can very well say, "I will not send my material to that location until you can show me that it has regained the 'passing' status." You might try to convince them, rightfully, that their material is not in grave danger of loss, but it might fall on deaf ears. Using the survey approach, the customer might feel as if you have seen the gaps and are making the adjustments. They still could have apprehension, but you may be able to show mitigating circumstances or conditions to help lessen their trepidation.

You may wish to consider both styles of measurement: one for internal and one for external consumption. You could have multiple assessment formats or tools developed to fit the style and classification of each operation. You also could have multiple styles contained in one instrument. A word of caution if you decide on a multifaceted implement: All the results are contained in that single document. If you pass the document in total or in part to a stakeholder, you might be giving them information that you would consider classified or proprietary.

6.9 Information Technology

Your information technology (IT) systems operating within the organization are the conduit to all your intended audiences to share, inform, instruct, monitor, and assess your supply chain security program. Companies of all types and in all industries rely heavily on their IT support and systems. They also rely on IT systems from other sources when sharing information or communicating data.

This is no different for your security program. You need to communicate with everyone whom the supply chain security program impacts or who requires support. You need it for research as well as distribution. We will not be talking of IT security in the traditional sense. Security applications of IT systems are complex and highly specialized tasks that are beyond the subject of this narrative. What we will be examining is how you effectively use IT programs and systems to implement, monitor, and enhance your supply security program.

One of the primary considerations for the use of IT in your program is how the IT system operates in your company. Who is allowed to have access to it? Are there different levels of access? How is it communicated throughout the organization? Is it communicated to computers only? Or additionally, are mobile devices or other electronic media connected? Another question to your IT group is the design of the network. Are VPNs (virtual private networks) and firewalls installed? Are there other filters in place? Is there access to the Internet?

You need to understand your organization's general application of IT so that you can better communicate your security programs. E-mails are a given. However, some IT systems block certain content that is transmitted through e-mail. If you are trying to send or receive a security assessment, you should ensure that it is compatible with your IT network. The same is true of embedded images and other nonwritten (typed) content. IT systems have myriad processes and filters in operation to detect a host of system-damaging programs. Your communication with other company locations, security providers, and Internet searches might touch on data that is interpreted by installed IT processes as potentially damaging. Constant and repetitive blocking of content and attachments can bring your ability to communicate security issues to a grinding halt.

Another tool in the IT kit for security's advantage is in regard to what media are available for training purposes. With the cost of travel and the disruption to operations when individuals are sent to off-site training, organizations have increased the use of IT-carried media for communication of training. Telephone conference calls are nearly as antique as the phonograph. They are still widely used, of course, but are very limiting in your ability to effectively communicate complex content.

Work with your IT group to see what they have in place, which could include video conferencing, web-based training programs, shared desktop applications, and e-learning programs. Some of these, like web-based and desktop sharing programs, are carried out in real time. You have an open line of communication of both audio and visual content. Others are programs and information stored for retrieval by others at random times. An e-learning program that offers the student exposure to specific content and also contains a validation component to determine that the content was sufficiently absorbed is a very effective training medium. One such type had the training blocked into modules or segments, and after each segment, there are select questions to answer. If the student does not show a predetermined proficiency, it will not allow the program to advance to the next module. Others add the testing phase at the end and track whether the student is able to obtain a minimum score. Failure to do so would require retraining.

The point of all this is that IT systems can carry the message and objectives of your security program as blood carries oxygen. Working closely with IT gives you access to all levels of activity and functions in the organization. It also gives them access to you for communication and transparency.

6.10 Liaisons

As the biblical saying goes, "Man cannot live by bread alone"; neither can your security program be effective without help, support, and input from other sources. If your program is to be contemporary and current with today's security risk conditions and environment, you must look outside your own knowledge base and understanding. Building liaisons and relationships with outside resources, groups, and entities affords you the opportunity of gaining information from them and working with them to enhance your program's effectiveness.

A good manager of any industry or function cannot expect to know everything. A good manager surrounds himself or herself with others who have expertise that augments what you know and what you need to complete your security mission and goals.

Another aspect of liaison building is the ability to reach out to other functions that can perform tasks outside your ability, resources, and authority. One of the most important in the world of supply chain security is law enforcement. Law enforcement is as concerned with theft of materials as you are. The best part is that they have far greater resources and authority to gain and utilize information than you. However, many times, it will be you or members of your security group who will supply valuable information to law enforcement in their duties of investigation and subsequent prosecution of criminal activity.

On the other hand, law enforcement (LE) can be a valuable asset of information for crime and criminal activity that may impact your company, its goods, or your client/customer's materials. When you are developing your security policies for the protection of the goods and materials, much of it is based on the knowledge of the risk and vulnerability in the environment in which you or they operate. Much of that information comes out of law enforcement. They see a greater picture of the criminal activities in an expansive region or area. Depending upon the jurisdiction of a particular LE group, their intimate knowledge base can be local, regional, national, or global.

LE also needs cooperation from your side. Often criminal activity is generated from your own employees, associates, providers, etc. When you are investigating an internal security incident, you look internally. Depending upon the circumstances, this internal investigation could lead to seeking LE cooperation and subsequent follow-up investigation. In other instances, LE may be working cases from their end, involving other companies (victims), but may need to look into people in your organization internally.

It is all about information sharing, even when you are not involved in an actual investigation. Your security program should include regular interaction with LE groups, security industry associations, associations that represent the transportation sectors—with anyone or anywhere that your security responsibilities intersect with your client's or customer's interests.

References

1. Dictionary of Business Terms, 2011. www.businessdictionary.com.
2. "Planning for Effective Communication," UC Berkley Finance and Administration Communication Guides, UC Berkeley, 2010. www.berkeley.edu.
3. F. John Reh, "Pareto's Principle—The 80–20 Rule: How the 80/20 Rule Can Help You Be More Effective," *About.Com/Management*. http://management.about.com/cs/generalmanagement/a/Pareto081202.htm.
4. Alex Lickerman, "Why We Need to Know Why: How Knowing the Reason for Things Shapes How We Respond to Them," 2010, *Psychology Today*. http://www.psychologytoday.com/blog/happiness-in-world/201011/why-we-need-know-why.
5. "A Few Ways to Master Business Change Management," Aveta Business Institute, April 28, 2011. www.sixsigmaonline.org/six-sigma-training-certification-information/a-few-ways-to-master-business-change-management-.html.
6. *Social Norms*, Sociology Guide, 2011. www.sociologyguide.com/basic-concepts/Social-Norms.php.
7. Ibid.

7

BUDGETING

Finally, we need to explore how all of this will be supported and financed. You will need to possess a firm understanding of how budgets work: how they are developed; the several types and styles of budgets; how they are funded, tracked, and analyzed. This chapter will not delve that deeply into the topic; however, we will consider the ways you might fund and manage the finances of your supply chain security program.

7.1 Justification

First, we need to look at who are you servicing with your security program. Throughout this book we have talked in general terms about your company, client, and customer interchangeably. This was done to illustrate the flexibility of your program, of how you can develop it for any number of uses, both internally and externally. When you think of budgeting or funding the program, this is a different story, in that the money needed to run the program has to have a source. Very basically, who will be paying for this security and how?

Then, it can be explained as two sections: internally and externally. Internally is what your company or client will provide for itself (*client*, meaning that you are their subject-matter expert [SME] or resident consultant to run their own supply chain security programs). The other, or the external program, will be what your providers have agreed or will be required to implement the security measures of your program.

The main difference between the two will be what portions or activities will be funded. The internal security program will cover the costs of the entire program. This means personnel, equipment, training, travel, communication expenses, and so on. If you are operating an external program, in that you have developed the security, but others are implementing it, then your focus is different. They will be financially responsible for all of their internal costs, and you will be responsible only for your portion of what it takes from your side to develop, monitor, adjust, and communicate with those who are actually executing the program's security measures. An internal program may also include financial support for security equipment and its installation, i.e., CCTV, access controls, and alarms. Externally, your cost would cover the travel and expense of inspecting another operation's CCTV, access controls, and alarms to ensure that they are following your security guidelines.

Of course, you will most likely be in a position of being responsible for a little of both. Your own company will be looking toward internal security measures as you develop and supply security for providers and others outside the company.

Budgets work on cycles. Some use the calendar year; others use 1 July or 1 September. Actually, they can use any date for the fiscal year. Many times the date is chosen to coincide with other reporting requirements they might be providing in the normal course of their business. In any case, your budget will be subject to that calendar. You should be sure to know these dates and know the budget-development timelines your company uses. Often the budget development begins six months prior to the beginning of the new fiscal year (FY). This gives a company time to develop, review, adjust, and eventually approve all of the budgets for all of the business units of the organization.

7.2 Internal versus External

For external supply chain security programs, the budget you develop will focus primarily on the costs associated with the monitoring and interaction with your providers and suppliers. Travel costs, communication costs (phones, Internet, etc.), and payroll for those who will be performing the interactions are all to be considered. Hopefully, you can capture this data from previous budgets and then project the activities required to provide a close estimate of the costs for the next fiscal year. If you are developing a Greenfield Supply Chain Security Program, then you will not be afforded the luxury of reviewing past expenses. If this is the case, consider networking with others in the industry on how they manage their budgets and what costs they experience. Most likely, your colleagues will not give you actual figures, but you can start to see how much time, travel, and other expenditures will be required to perform the many tasks associated with your program. Your organization will probably have established guidelines on some costs that will provide you with the numbers you need. As an example, many companies use a service for booking and management of travel. These companies are a resource for estimated costs associated with the travel you or your managers will experience. Other line items to consider are rent (for office space), office supplies, training and equipment, IT costs, and conference/seminar/professional development.

For internal programs, you will need to include most, if not all, of the previously mentioned budgetary considerations. In addition, an internal program requires equipment: CCTV, access control systems, alarms, etc. For supply chain security work, you have to ask yourself a question. The answer to this question will also depend upon the profit and loss (P&L) structure of your organization, namely, who pays for what and who is responsible for covering direct operating expenses (DOEs) and has P&L responsibility. The question is simply, "Who is paying for this equipment?" Some organizations place all DOEs as well as the expenses for building and support systems with the manager of the facility. This means that the expense of even a light-bulb has its accounting along with the location that uses the lightbulb. They determine what they need; they agree on an acceptable price (that may be regulated by company policy, which is good to know here, too); they make the purchase; and they install and maintain. All of these costs impact the profitability of the operation as dictated and allowed under the company's financial policies and procedures. An example of a P&L-based budget is given in Appendix D.

Another often seen method is a shared system. You will develop an item in your budget to identify, purchase, and install required equipment. Then, once installed, you turn the security systems over to the location management. They then become responsible for maintenance of the systems. Location managers love this, since they do not need to worry about the initial cost, which could be substantial for larger footprints. Security managers do not like this system, since now you have to try to predict usage and project the costs of the equipment and installations, which are also substantial.

The better system is the P&L-based plan. It is far easier to control costs based on need—as needed and when needed. Location managers will try to minimize the need, since they are paying, but with your guidance, you can supply an efficacious security program to service their needs. Plus, if they paid for it, they will tend to maintain it better.

7.3 Own or Rent?

An additional note I associate with budgeting equipment is buying versus leasing. There are advantages for both. Both can be included in the budget: leasing for the length of the contract and purchase as an initial cost amortized over the life of the products.

Leasing is an acceptable method if you do not plan on being at that location for more than three to five years. If there is a move or closure of the location, the equipment is retrieved, and the cancellation costs are minimal. For purchased systems, moving or closing will entail taking the equipment to the new location, which is a cost savings for the new location. If there is not another location identified, the equipment can be stored for future use or sold off to recover some of the initial costs, or passed on to the landlord or new tenants of the location. For locations that plan on staying for more than the three- to five-year period, then a purchase plan makes good sense. The purchaser will receive the benefit of the equipment for a long period of time well past the amortized ending date.

A word to the wise on leasing: Read the contract. When you negotiate the leasing agreement and determine a yearly cost for budgeting, look at the ending date and see how that affects the agreement. Be wary of automatic rollovers. Some verbiage says that there is a thirty-day window for ending the lease prior to the expiration of the lease. If the end date comes and goes, the lease will automatically renew for a specified period from a year to as much as five years more. There is usually a cost increase automatically included. If you try to break the lease after the renew date, you could be charged for the remainder of the time on the lease agreement. It is a hard sell to your finance people to spend money on a system you do not even have. This goes for maintenance and monitoring service agreements as well.

PART III

REGULATION AND RESOURCE

8

GOVERNMENT AND INDUSTRY SUPPLY CHAIN SECURITY PROGRAMS

The following section will illustrate the expansiveness and importance of supply chain security. You will find that when you review and familiarize yourself with the dozens of government-sponsored supply chain security programs, you may notice one of two things. Either their program looks a lot like yours, or yours may look a lot like theirs. This is a good thing. In fact, depending upon the nature of the work or industry of your client, the type of material it handles, and the regions in which it operates, your supply chain security program should be compatible with if not compliant to these directives.

If you are tasked with a Greenfield-type build of a supply chain security program, you will be able to gain a lot of insight and direction for your policies and procedures right from the pages of these government documents. If you are taking over an already existing program, then it will be critical that you compare the existing security to these programs that may be mandated for compliance. Any incongruent information or matter you find will require adjustment and modification.

A word of caution: These programs are constantly evolving. As the environment of supply chain security changes, so will these programs. Today, these programs were primarily developed to counteract terrorist activity. Originally, many of these programs began with anti-organized crime or anti-smuggling agendas. With the advent of regional and global terrorist activity that may target the legitimate supply chain, the policies, protocols, and procedures were modified and enlarged to encompass these threats. As these change, so should your program. Some programs, you will see, require regular reporting and updating. Others do not, but assume that you are aware of their changes, and amend your affected policies and adjust them accordingly. Failure to be diligent in your monitoring could have severe consequences. Some programs can limit the movement of your client's material; another may have the authority to fine your company thousands of dollars, euros, yen, etc. Still others have jurisdiction over licensing that your client or company may need to operate within a region or nation.

The following sections describe the more prevalent programs. The covered programs are not all inclusive. As discussed previously, you have a responsibility to investigate and learn what government or industry regulations or guidelines exist in any region or area where your company, client, provider, supplier, or customer may operate.

8.1 C-TPAT (Customs-Trade Partnership against Terrorism)

C-TPAT seeks to safeguard the world's vibrant trade industry from terrorists, maintaining the economic health of the United States and its neighbors. The partnership develops and adopts measures that add security but do not have a chilling effect on trade, a difficult balancing act.

8.1.1 A Growing Partnership

Begun in November 2001 with just seven major importers as members, the partnership has grown. As of June 2011, more than 10,000 certified partners that run the gamut of the trade community have been accepted into the program. These include U.S. importers, U.S./Canada highway carriers; U.S./Mexico highway carriers; rail and sea carriers; licensed U.S. Customs brokers; U.S. marine port authority/terminal operators; U.S. freight consolidators; ocean transportation intermediaries and nonoperating common carriers; Mexican and Canadian manufacturers; and Mexican long-haul carriers. These 10,000+ companies account for over 50% (by value) of what is imported into the United States.

8.1.2 Extending the Zone of U.S. Border Security

By extending the United States' zone of security to the point of origin, the customs-trade partnership allows for better risk assessment and targeting, freeing the U.S. Customs and Border Patrol (CBP) to allocate inspectional resources to more questionable shipments.

The partnership establishes clear supply chain security criteria for members to meet, and in return, it provides incentives and benefits like expedited processing. A corollary is to extend the partnership antiterrorism principles globally through cooperation and coordination with the international community. In 2005, the World Customs Organization (WCO) adopted the Framework of Standards to Secure and Facilitate Global Trade, which complements and globalizes CBP's and the partnership's cargo security efforts.

8.1.3 How It Works

When they join the antiterror partnership, companies sign an agreement to work with CBP to protect the supply chain, identify security gaps, and implement specific security measures and best practices. Additionally, partners provide CBP with a security profile outlining the specific security measures the company has in place. Applicants must address a broad range of security topics and present security profiles that list action plans to align security throughout their supply chain.

C-TPAT members are considered low risk and are therefore less likely to be examined. This designation is based on a company's past compliance history, security profile, and the validation of a sample international supply chain.

8.1.4 An Emerging Focus: Mutual Recognition Arrangements

CBP has numerous mutual recognition arrangements with other countries. The goal of these arrangements is to link the various international industry partnership programs so that together they create a unified and sustainable security posture that can assist in securing and facilitating global cargo trade (http://www.cbp.gov/xp/cgov/trade/cargo_security/ctpat).

8.2 PIP (Partners in Protection)

Partners in Protection (PIP) is a Canada Border Services Agency (CBSA) program that enlists the cooperation of private industry to enhance border and trade chain security, combat organized crime and terrorism, and help detect and prevent contraband smuggling.

It is a voluntary program with no membership fee that aims to secure the trade chain, one partnership at a time. PIP members agree to implement and adhere to high security standards, while the CBSA agrees to assess their security measures, provide information sessions on security issues, and offer other benefits. Member companies are recognized as being trusted traders, which allows the CBSA to focus its resources on areas of higher or unknown risk.

Through their partnership with the CBSA, PIP members contribute to the security of the supply chain and the facilitation of legitimate trade.

8.2.1 History

Partners in Protection (PIP) was developed in 1995 with a primary focus on promoting business awareness and compliance with customs regulations. After the events of 9/11, the PIP program's focus shifted to place a greater emphasis on trade chain security, which included urging members to improve their physical, infrastructural, and procedural security. A security questionnaire was developed with suggested security recommendations.

The importance of the PIP program increased in 2002, when a PIP membership became a prerequisite to participate in the Free and Secure Trade (FAST) program. FAST provides expedited border clearances into Canada for preapproved importers, carriers, and drivers.

8.2.2 Modernization

On June 30, 2008, a strengthened PIP program was implemented with: minimum security requirements; mandatory site validations; denial, suspension, cancellation, reinstatement, and appeal policies and procedures; and an automated application process.

These steps have ensured that PIP is aligned with international standards such as the Framework of Standards to Secure and Facilitate

Global Trade (SAFE) of the World Customs Organization, which includes guidelines for Authorized Economic Operators. It also set the stage for PIP to enter into mutual recognition arrangements with similar programs in other countries.

8.2.3 Mutual Recognition

Mutual recognition arrangements (MRAs) between PIP and compatible customs-trade partnership programs expand the international trade network of accredited low-risk companies. The MRA signifies that both countries apply similar security standards and similar site validations when approving companies for membership in their respective programs, and that both countries recognize each others' members and may grant them similar benefits.

MRAs allow customs administrations to work together to improve their capability to target high-risk shipments while expediting legitimate cargo. To enhance cross-border security, the CBSA has signed MRAs recognizing the compatibility of its PIP program with the following foreign programs:

June 2008: U.S. Customs and Border Protection—Customs-Trade Partnership against Terrorism (C-TPAT) program

June 2010: Japan Customs and Tariff Bureau—Authorized Economic Operator (AEO) program

June 2010: Korea Customs Service—Authorized Economic Operator (AEO) program

June 2010: Singapore Customs—Secure Trade Partnership (STP) program

8.2.4 Harmonization of PIP and C-TPAT

The similarity between PIP's and C-TPAT's security requirements makes it easier to apply for membership in both programs (a separate application form must be submitted to each program). Only one site validation may be necessary for applicants to both PIP and C-TPAT. However, both programs reserve the right to perform site validations and site revalidations.

PIP members can also benefit from expedited border clearance into Canada if they apply for and are approved by the Free and

Secure Trade (FAST) program to use the FAST lanes into Canada. Remember that to apply for FAST entry into Canada, membership in both the Customs Self-Assessment program and PIP is required.

In November 2009, Canada and the United States announced initiatives to streamline cross-border shipping, including the alignment of the PIP and C-TPAT programs. PIP and C-TPAT are collaborating on a single application process for those applying to both programs and are examining the standardization of their policies and procedures and the sharing of information (http://www.cbsa-asfc.gc.ca).

8.3 FAST (Free and Secure Trade)

This program is a commercial clearance program designed to ensure safety and security while expediting legitimate trade across the Canada–U.S. border. FAST is a joint initiative between the Canada Border Services Agency (CBSA) and U.S. Customs and Border Protection that enhances border and trade chain security while making cross-border commercial shipments simpler and subject to fewer delays.

It is a voluntary program that enables the CBSA to work closely with the private sector to enhance border security, combat organized crime and terrorism, and prevent contraband smuggling. Under the U.S. Western Hemisphere Travel Initiative, FAST members who are Canadian or U.S. citizens can use their FAST membership card as an alternative document to the passport when entering the United States by land or water. Permanent residents of Canada or the United States still require a passport and visa (if applicable) to enter the United States.

The CBSA and industry are mutually committed to maintaining the FAST program requirements, and they work together to achieve compliance and to find solutions to problems.

8.3.1 How It Works

All FAST program participants (drivers, carriers, and importers) must undergo a risk assessment. FAST-approved participants are identified as low risk, which enables the CBSA to focus its resources and security efforts on travelers of high or unknown risk.

When a FAST-approved driver arrives at the border, he or she presents three bar-coded documents to the border services officer (one for each of the participating parties: the driver, the carrier, and the importer). The officer can quickly scan the bar codes while all trade data declarations and verifications are done at a later time, away from the border.

Under FAST, eligible goods arriving for approved companies and transported by approved carriers using registered drivers are cleared into Canada or the United States with greater speed and certainty, which reduces costs for FAST participants.

Also, as of November 25, 2009, FAST members can use their FAST membership card as proof of identity and citizenship to enter Canada in all lanes, including regular highway lanes, even in a non-commercial vehicle. Dedicated FAST lanes have been established at a number of major border crossings.

8.3.2 Benefits

- You gain access to dedicated lanes (where available) for faster and more efficient border clearance.
- In all highway lanes, including the regular, nondedicated lanes, you can use your FAST membership card as proof of identity and a document that denotes citizenship when entering Canada.
- FAST is a streamlined process that reduces delivery times and landed costs of imports.
- There is no need to transmit transactional data for every transaction.
- Minimal documentation is required to clear the border.
- FAST provides increased certainty at the border, resulting in fewer delays.
- FAST is a unified, ongoing partnership with the CBSA.
- The program promotes Canadian competitiveness.
- The program advances voluntary compliance and self-assessment.

8.3.3 FAST-Eligible Goods

In order to qualify for the streamlined FAST process, goods imported into Canada must meet these conditions (http://www.cbsa-asfc.gc.ca):

- They must not be prohibited, controlled, or regulated importations as set out in any act of Parliament or provincial legislation.
- They must not be subject to the release requirements of any other government department.
- They must be shipped directly to Canada from the continental United States or Mexico.

8.4 BASC (Business Alliance for Secure Commerce)

BASC is a business–customs partnership created to promote safe international trade in cooperation with governments and international organizations. The World BASC Organization (WBO) is constituted as a nonprofit organization under the laws of the state of Delaware. The WBO is led by the private sector, whose mission is to secure and facilitate international trade by the establishment and administration of global security standards and procedures applied to the supply chain of international trade.

Global business organizations that are committed to working together on the common purpose of strengthening international trade through the implementation of internationally recognized security standards and procedures may join this organization. The following mission and vision statements as well as the specific objectives are from the BASC website (http://www.wbasco.org/english/what_is_basc.htm).

8.4.1 Mission

"Facilitate and promote world trade by establishing and administrating global supply chain security standards and procedures, in partnership with business, governments, customs, law enforcement agencies and international business organizations."

8.4.2 Vision

"Recognized world leaders in securing and facilitating international trade through management of security standards to be implemented by companies in coordination with countries, customs administrations and international institutions and organizations."

8.4.3 Specific Objectives

The BASC general objective is to promote secure international trade. Specific objectives are:

- Motivate a security culture and protection to international trade.
- Establish and administer a control and security management system for the supply chain.
- Work in coordination with governments and international organizations.
- Promote strategic partnerships.
- Generate confidence and credibility between governments and businesses.
- Strengthen cooperation between private sector and government.

8.5 AEO (Authorized Economic Operator)

One of the main elements of the security amendment of the Community Customs Code (Regulation [EC] 648/2005) is the creation of the AEO concept. On the basis of Article 5a of the security amendments, member states can grant the AEO status to any economic operator meeting the following common criteria: customs compliance, appropriate record keeping, financial solvency and, where relevant, security and safety standards.

The status of "authorized economic operator" granted by one member state is recognized by the other member states. This does not automatically allow them to benefit from simplifications provided for in the customs rules in the other member states. However, other member states should grant the use of simplifications to authorized economic operators if they meet specific requirements.

Economic operators can apply for an AEO status either to have easier access to customs simplifications or to be in a more favorable position to comply with the new security requirements. Under the security framework, which has been applicable since July 1, 2009, economic operators have to submit pre-arrival and pre-departure information on goods entering or leaving the European Union (EU). The security type of AEO certificate and the combined one allow their holders to benefit from facilitations with regard to the new customs controls relating to security.

The detailed provisions are laid down in the amendment of the Implementing Provisions of the Community Customs Code. These provisions were drafted on the basis of experiences from the AEO Pilot conducted in 2006. Regulation (EC) 197/2010 has established new time limits for issuing the AEO certificate.

Regulation (EC) 1192/2008 aligns the rules for granting both the AEO certificate for customs simplifications and the single authorization for simplified procedures (SASP). Being an AEO facilitates the process of achieving a single authorization for simplified procedures, as the relevant criteria are deemed to be met.

8.5.1 AEO Guidelines

The AEO guidelines ensure harmonized implementation of the AEO rules throughout the EU, guaranteeing the equal treatment of economic operators and transparency of the rules. Part One of the AEO guidelines explains the AEO concept based on the adopted legislation, including:

- Explanations about the different categories of AEO
- A specific section dedicated to small- and medium-sized enterprises (SMEs) with guidance on how to examine the AEO requirements if the applicant is an SME
- A section giving advice to customs authorities on how to speed up the authorization process
- Guidance for both customs authorities and trade on how to facilitate the procedure for parent/subsidiary companies
- A description of the AEO benefits with indications on the relevant AEO category and on the time frame for the application of particular benefit
- A complete explanation on the concept of "business partners' security"
- An explanation, with concrete examples, for determining the competent member state where the AEO application has to be submitted
- Guidelines for multinational companies and large businesses

- Guidance on how to perform monitoring after an AEO certificate has been issued

Part Two contains the questionnaire, providing a list of points to assist both customs authorities and AEO applicants in assessing whether or not the AEO criteria are met. For information and copies of related and referenced documents, see the European Commission's website (http://ec.europa.eu).

8.6 CCSP (Certified Cargo Screening Program)

8.6.1 Background

CCSP is a Transportation Security Administration (TSA)–regulated program developed as a result of a congressional mandate. In 2007, Congress passed the Implementing Recommendations of the 9/11 Commission Act, more commonly known as the 9/11 Act. This law requires that all cargo transported on a passenger aircraft be screened for explosives as of August 1, 2010.

TSA continues to encourage businesses to closely examine how they ship cargo on passenger aircraft. TSA recognizes that cargo may only be a small portion of your operation, but all businesses must consider how the new requirement has affected their operational continuity, punctuality, and customer satisfaction.

Every shipment of cargo carried on passenger aircraft requires screening at piece level prior to being transported on any passenger aircraft. Skids and pallets will have to be taken apart, screened, and reconfigured. The 9/11 Act specifically identifies the types of screening allowed, ranging from physical inspection to various technologies. If airlines are forced to screen cargo, similar to how passenger baggage is screened, there is a potential for delays and damage to shipments. The screening process affects all cargo on passenger planes.

TSA developed the Certified Cargo Screening Program (CCSP) as a solution to help industry reach the 100% screening mandate. The program enables freight forwarders and shippers to prescreen cargo prior to arrival at the airport. Most CCSP shipper participants have been able to quickly incorporate physical screening into their shipping process at a small cost to their operation.

TSA continues working with companies to examine all their cargo screening options. Shippers should contact their freight forwarders to determine if any of their products are transported on passenger aircraft. Many freight forwarders have already joined CCSP, and in many cases will be able to help companies through the screening process.

TSA can assist in assessing the possible impact for your supply chain, both inbound from suppliers as well as outbound customer shipments. However, there are also certain products that are better suited to being screened by the shippers themselves. TSA will help with these decisions, and companies should consider contacting them for more details on CCSP at TSA.gov.

8.6.2 Program Overview

Under CCSP, TSA certifies cargo-screening facilities located throughout the United States to screen cargo prior to providing it to airlines for shipment on passenger flights. Participation in the program is voluntary and is designed to enable vetted, validated, and certified supply chain facilities to comply with the 100% screening requirement.

CCSP is a practical supply chain solution that provides security while ensuring the flow of commerce. Cargo is screened at the most efficient and effective point. It is done before individual pieces of cargo are consolidated for shipment.

Certified Cargo Screening Facilities (CCSF) must carry out a TSA-approved security program and adhere to strict chain-of-custody requirements. Cargo must be secured from the time it is screened until it is placed on passenger aircraft for shipment.

8.6.3 Benefits

Screening 100% of cargo on passenger aircraft is designed to ensure the safety of the traveling public. TSA designed CCSP to provide businesses with the option to screen cargo in a cost-effective manner and at various points of the supply chain.

CCSP allows businesses to

- Screen cargo where it is packaged
- Maintain in-house packaging integrity

- Avoid screening logjams at the airport
- Build bulk configurations to minimize cost

A CCSP program

- Is supported by the air-freight and air-carrier industries
- Leverages best practices from global supply chain programs
- Allows businesses to choose the best and most effective model for their needs

(See TSA website at www.tsa.gov/what_we_do/tsnm/air_cargo/programs.shtm.)

8.7 TAPA (Transported Asset Protection Association)

TAPA is a private-industry organization that was originally founded with the intent to develop more stringent supply chain security for the transportation and handling of high-tech materials and goods. It has evolved to developing these procedures for any type of high-value, high-risk product. Many technology, pharmaceutical, and other high-value and high-risk product companies have incorporated some, or nearly all, of the security guidelines in their own supply chain security program, with which they also require their transportation providers, handlers, and distributors to be in compliance.

8.7.1 About TAPA

When you join TAPA, you're aligning your company or organization with an internationally recognized leader in the fight against cargo crime.

TAPA AMERICAS represents one of three primary branches of TAPA worldwide—the other two being TAPA EMEA (Europe and Africa) and TAPA APAC (Asia/Pacific). These branches include chapters in South Africa and Mexico, with new chapters developing in other countries plagued by cargo crime. Each TAPA branch or chapter participates in the worldwide organization while also addressing the needs of its own regional members.

8.7.2 HVTT Asset Theft: A Shared Problem

HVTT (high-value theft targeted) asset theft poses a major problem for many industries. Theft of electronics, pharmaceuticals, clothing, high-end foodstuffs, auto parts, building supplies, and almost any other cargo of value is a daily event in the Americas. This type of crime leads to billions of dollars in lost revenue, compromised brand integrity, and in some cases harm to consumers. While government programs such as C-TPAT focus on keeping dangerous items out of the supply chain, TAPA focuses mainly on the issue of theft. But because the concerns are interrelated, TAPA and government agencies work together in confronting these challenges.

8.7.3 Standards Lead to Solutions

The leverage TAPA exerts has had a measurably positive impact in promoting standardization and industry change to reduce cargo crime (http://tapaonline.org):

- Major freight handlers are joining TAPA or employing TAPA-recognized security standards for facility certification as well as for freight care and handling.
- TAPA has become a worldwide benchmark for security handling guidelines and practices.
- Businesses insurers are asking prospective customers about their security practices, and specifically whether they hold TAPA certification.
- Government agencies include TAPA-endorsed standards in their development of homeland security initiatives.

9

RESOURCES AND TECHNOLOGY FOR SUPPLY CHAIN SECURITY

There are many tools of the trade for utilization within your supply chain security program. Many of them have been on the market and in use for years. Many of them have dual use for other industries or functions as well as security.

Being current within the security industry and its organizations and associations provides a conduit to current and developing technologies and applications of devices, systems, and protocols. We mentioned previously that building a relationship with other industries and functional groups offers insight into their challenges and solutions. There are always other actions from another nonsecurity-related function or group that could have a procedure, method, or appliance that could have innovative security applications.

The following examples show some of the security solutions that are available. Many are well known; others may not be, yet they still have relevant security applications.

9.1 GPS (Global Positioning System)

GPS is a well-known system with both commercial and private uses. It sends out a signal that is received by satellite and is bounced back to the device. It tracks location and movement. The signals, or pings, can be adjusted to be rapid for near-pinpoint tracking or to greater gaps for less intensity. You see it is personal vehicles; it is available for marine use; and there are even small devices for tracking junior when he says he is "at the mall." Its use in commercial trucking helps to track valuable loads for security. It also helps in dispatching and fleet management.

GPS devices are easily introduced into material for security tracking when moved by truck, rail, or ocean. As of the writing of this book, GPS is not allowed on commercial airlines that fly material or cargo. The airline industry is examining the use of GPS, since it feels that because such devices emit a signal, they might interfere with air communications or other systems. Many of the devices on the market today can integrate environmental conditions of the material, as well.

9.2 GSM (Global System for Mobile Communications)

GSM is a popular standard for mobile phones, used vastly across the world. According to the estimates made by the GSM Association, the promoter of GSM, 80% of the global market uses the GSM-standard mobile phones. In GSM-enabled mobile phones, the signaling and speech channels are digital, and thus it is regarded as a second generation (or 2G) mobile phone system.

Different from GPS, which depends upon satellite positioning, "the GSM mobile phone tracking system, more often referred to as GSM localization, is a cell phone tower and network tracking system which uses the hyperbolic [cell tower triangulation] positioning process to determine the exact location of a GSM enabled cell phone, thus indirectly tracking its user. In hyperbolic positioning, a particular object is accurately located by computing the time difference in arrival of the signals that are emitted from the object to three or more receivers" (http://www.darkgovernment.com/news/how-gsm-mobile-phone-tracking-works).

There are three methods of GSM mobile phone tracking:

- Network-based mobile phone tracking system
- Handset-based mobile phone tracking system
- Hybrid mobile phone tracking system

9.3 Trucking-Focused Devices

Besides GPS-type tracking used in the trucking industry, there are also other devices that can be utilized for enhancing security. The most common are seals, but not the simple seal to determine if a load was entered or compromised. These can range from inexpensive tin or plastic strips to "bolt" seals (see Figure 9.1). There are seal systems that can both indicate entry as well as lock down the container.

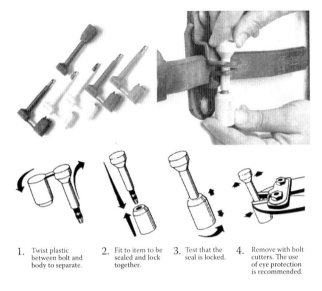

1. Twist plastic between bolt and body to separate.   2. Fit to item to be sealed and lock together.   3. Test that the seal is locked.   4. Remove with bolt cutters. The use of eye protection is recommended.

Figure 9.1   Typical bolt seal. (Photo courtesy Ray Fernandez, Sealock.)

Bolt seals are very durable, and one needs a bolt cutter or a similar tool to remove them. They help to lock down the doors or hatches as well. There are other systems that have protective coverings over the seal that requires a specifically designed tool to remove the covering and seal. To otherwise remove this would take cutting torches or reciprocating saws. This takes time and brings unwanted attention to the material and the vehicle.

Another is the kill switch. GPS can be integrated with the ability to shut off the vehicle either through the ignition module or by shutting down the fuel pumps, thus immobilizing the vehicle. If considering this type of truck device, find out if local laws allowed it. Many jurisdictions do not allow this, since it can immobilize a truck while traveling on a road or highway, thereby endangering people or causing significant traffic congestion.

9.4 Asset Tracking and Radio Frequency Identification (RFID)

This function has been in use for many years at many levels. For supply chain security, you would look to this as a way to isolate the material at any single point along the chain. You want to be able to say that the goods have been sent at a point and received at a point.

Optimally, you are looking to verify all of the material at any location. It also assists with inventory management and ownership identification. Identification tagging is the most popular. Companies attach company-unique descriptors to corporate assets. They may show the corporate name or just bar or alphanumeric codes. These are tracked as assets of the company, assignments to groups, functions, or individuals. It aids in the allocation of the items, inventory, depreciation of the asset, and antitheft deterrence.

Other technologies are bar coding and RFID (radio frequency identification), which are already popular and global asset tracking systems. These allow for instant and real-time verification and documentation of material specifics, quality, and quantity. Bar coding is seen in use across all industries, from asset tracking to consumer uses of inventory management to consumer purchasing processes and habits. You would be hard-pressed to find a product that is not associated with a bar code either in its packaging or directly integrated with the item itself. Shipping labels with bar coding allow for handoff of entire containers all the way down to individual pieces in the supply chain. It all depends upon what level you wish to verify. Scanning of the bar codes can be done automatically, as in the handling of airline baggage (see Figure 9.2a) or in the letter and parcel business, or it can

Figure 9.2a   Airline baggage handling.

Figure 9.2b   Handheld scanning.

consist of hand scanning, with workers utilizing a handheld device (see Figure 9.2b) aimed at specific pieces. The information from the bar code is stored for later download or fed back into databases for comparisons and verification information.

RFID is an excellent technology for the tracking of material goods and products through the supply chain, offering clear segmentation of the chain at all handoffs from introduction at origin to delivery to the end user. It consists an automatic reader of the RFID tag that can report on the specifics of the tagged item(s) as it passes through the RFID gateway. One of the reasons that RFID is so popular is that it can read numerous tags and, therefore, numerous items at a single pass. RFID tags can be applied to the container and the piece simultaneously. When passing through a portal, it will read all of the tagged items. Depending upon the capability of the database, it could indicate immediately if any piece was not read, which could be considered as missing. This is of particular interest to your supply chain security program for detection of theft or pilferage. All of this information is fed back into databases for tracking and comparisons of information.

Primarily, there are two types of RFID systems: active and passive. Active RFID requires an energy source at the tag level. It will have a battery or energy source of some type that emits a signal. A reader will then pick up this signal and read the information associated with that tag for later use (see Figure 9.3). The downside of an active system is that the energy sources, typically batteries, are consumed, and when this happens, they lose their ability to track the item or material to which they are attached. You see this type of technology for bridge and highway tolls in many countries. The tag is attached to a high point in the front portion of the vehicle, and overhead readers pick up the signals as the vehicle passes under or within a designated proximity. When the battery is exhausted, either the battery or the tag

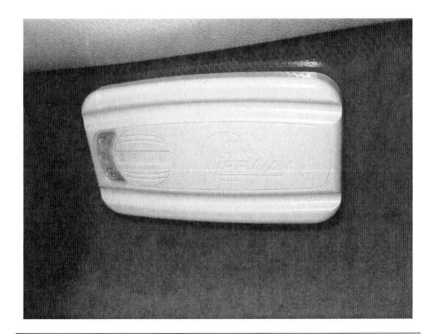

Figure 9.3 RFID—active.

is easily replaced. The tags are used over and over again as long as an energy source is supplied or renewed.

The other RFID system, passive RFID, is typically used for single-purpose tracking and is considered disposable. The tag is merely an antenna that reflects a signal from a transmitter back to the transmitter or another antenna for reading of the associated information. They are very small, lightweight tags without any energy or battery required. They can be embedded into labels, packaging, and other devices that are attached or applied to just about any type of material you wish to track and verify.

Many consumer industries use passive RFID to track their goods into their inventory, which is useful in management of the inventory, including distribution and eventual sales. It is easy to use, since the tag only needs to be placed in a specified vicinity of the reader. Popular uses are in grocery and department stores as well as parts and product suppliers, etc. Look at an RFID tag closely and you will note the presence of a metallic substance or a circuitry-like pattern, which is the reflective antenna (see Figure 9.4).

Unfortunately, there are some limitations in the deployment of RFID, either active or passive. Of special note is when the commodities are

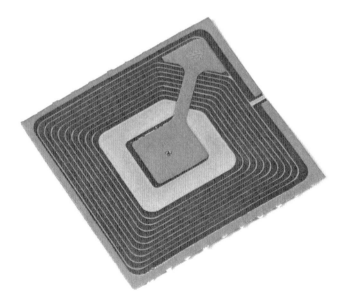

Figure 9.4　RFID—passive, with embedded antenna.

mixed or there are other service providers or handlers in the transportation and distribution of the material. In either system, there are a number of supporting systems. This means that there are many different types of readers, tags, and databases. For the application to be effective, the systems need to be compatible. When setting up an RFID tracking system, the organization needs to agree on the type (active/passive) required, the style of tags that will be used, appropriate reader or portal systems to be installed, and how the databases will interact with the system, and even how the information might be shared with others, if required.

If you are running a passive, label-embedded RFID technology, your system, RFID type, frequency, portals/readers, and databases will all need to be compatible at any point you wish to document the movement of the material. This could be within a distribution location or anywhere in your supply chain, locally, regionally, or globally.

In the event that your RFID-tagged material is handled or transported by a provider that might utilize a different system, your tags will not be read, and you will not have the transparency that RFID provides.

9.5 Taping/Wrapping

One effective supply chain security technique to prevent pilferage, the introduction of substances, or contamination of material is to place a barrier between the material and the outside world. When a container or product is well wrapped or contained, it not only keeps the product secure inside, it also prevents others from penetrating the external packaging and accessing the internal material. In some instances, the packaging is integral to the product as a container used to protect the item and provides a container for handling and shipping as well.

In other uses, and industries, items are wrapped to help facilitate the handling when being transported. A stack of loose tires is far more manageable if wrapped with a plastic than to have them simply stacked on a skid (see Figure 9.5). At the same time, if these tires, which can be very highly valued and at risk for theft, are wrapped effectively, they have to be handled well, and the contents must be isolated from the outside world and those who might be looking to target such goods.

If packed loose, one or two missing tires might not be detected until far down the supply chain. If wrapped, it could become obvious at a handoff that there has been an attack on the shipment.

Figure 9.5   Clear shrink-wrapping.

The cargo and logistics industry has widespread use of this technique. Companies who decide to wrap for protection, as well as handling, sometimes decide to use an opaque colored wrap, such as black. This prohibits others from seeing what kinds of goods or material are in the container or on the skid. There is some controversy surrounding this technique. If there is black wrap around a skid of material, it could indicate that the goods are of high value and can be targeted for further inspection (by the criminals) or possibly a *shopping theft*: "Let's just hit it or take it anyway, as it probably is something we can sell to somebody."

An additional wrapping method for enhanced security is security taping. Once the material is wrapped, an additional layer or application of tape is applied over the wrap. The tape used is security tape

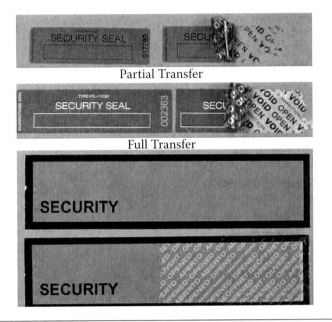

Partial Transfer

Full Transfer

SECURITY

SECURITY

Figure 9.6   Tamper-evident tape.

in that it is tamper-evident technology (TET) (see Figure 9.6). TET tape will indicate if the tape has been moved or removed from the wrap by leaving a residue on the wrapping material. There are many types of TET security tape. Some leave a colored residue, other will leave actual alphanumeric indicators that there has been tampering.

In any case, the security tape is most effective when applied across all planes of the material: sides, top, corners, edging, etc. (see Figure 9.7). Even if the wrapping itself is torn or lifted, the security tape will stretch or break, and the TET component will be observed.

9.6 Seals

Seals afford two main purposes. The first is to indicate if there has been any entry into a container. The other is to keep honest people honest. Sealed does not mean locked, even though there are some seal systems that can perform both functions. Primarily, a seal is applied to indicate that the material within the container, device, or truck has been verified and documented, and that upon handoff or reception at the next phase of handling, it is still in that same condition. This is quite important for products that are climate or environmentally

Figure 9.7   Security-tape application.

sensitive or at a contamination risk if there is an uncontrolled or unauthorized opening of the container. It is not to indicate a theft, but to ensure the condition of the material from point to point.

Seals are also a supply chain security measure. Once verified and documented, the sealed shipment has an expectation that all items and material contained therein remain so during its travel through the supply chain. A missing or tampered seal is an indicator that there could have been an unauthorized entry into the truck and that some or all of the goods in the truck could be missing, prompting further investigation.

Seals are best applied for shipments that go directly from point to point. That is, the container or truck is loaded and sealed, and is not opened again until destination. It will be at that point the seal will be verified and broken. Transits that make multiple stops along the way are less than ideal for seal applications.

Most seals used in industry are relatively simple devices made of plastic or metal strips (see Figure 9.8). There are also simple placard seals that are placed over seams or hinges of doors or hatch-type enclosures. These also are designed with TET, so that if the door is opened and/or the seal is disturbed, residue or other material will indicate tampering (see Figure 9.6). Overall, they are well suited for the purpose of documentation and entry detection.

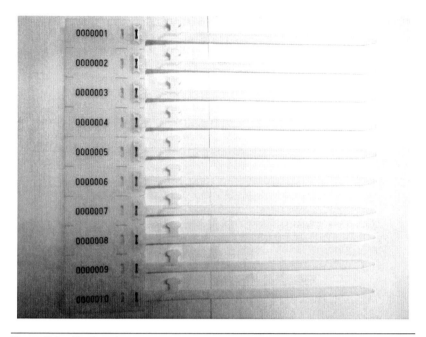

Figure 9.8   Plastic seals.

Then there are seals that have a dual purpose of being a security locking device as well as a verification tool. These are seals created to assist in hardening of the target and to enhance the resistance and effort in accessing the container's contents. One such popular seal is the *bolt seal* (see Figure 9.1). The bolt seal is aptly named, as it is constructed in a fashion similar to a regular bolt-type fastening device. Usually about three inches long and made of high strength steel, once applied, it must be cut off using bolt cutters or some sort of metal-cutting saw. Tests on bolt seals have shown that they are highly resistant to prying or other means of removal. If there is an attempt to remove the bolt seal, the damage is evident. Outfitted with bolt cutters or effective pry tools, the criminal can easily remove the seal, also. However you must possess these tools at the time of entry. The bolt seal can deter the criminal who is not prepared for this barrier. It is both a locking-type device as well as a documentation seal, but it should not be considered a highly secure or highly durable locking device. Many regional and international customs agencies required bolt-type seals for security containers or trucks that cross borders or other regulated transit locations. Wire or cable seals are also a viable alternative to bolt-seal technology and application (see Figure 9.9).

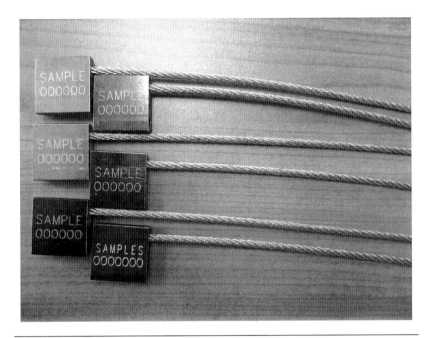

Figure 9.9 Wire seals. (Photo courtesy Ray Fernandez, Sealock.)

Other seal and lock mechanisms have durable metal bars or coverings that provide great resistance to unauthorized entry. By design, the composition and design of the metallic components permanently interlock (see Figure 9.10). Bolt cutters and pry bars and standard cutting tools are ineffective against its hardiness. After application, only specialized tools specifically made for the sealing device

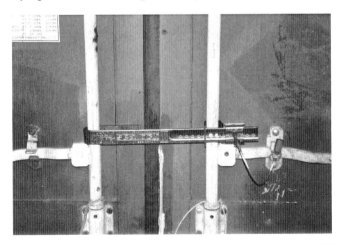

Figure 9.10 Bar seal. (Photo courtesy Ray Fernandez, Sealock.)

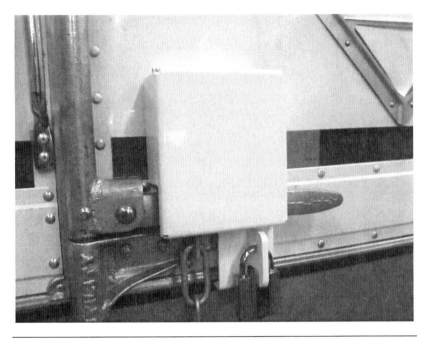

Figure 9.11   Seal cover. (Photo courtesy Ray Fernandez, Sealock.)

or high-output cutters, like acetylene torches or high-speed metal saws, are able to remove the seal. Most companies and transportation industries consider these to be high-security seals.

Seal-producing companies have also devised and market steel devices that cover the seal and lock mechanisms. So not only do you have to deal with cutting a durable seal system, you have to cut through an outer cover just to gain access to the inner seal (see Figure 9.11).

9.7 Screening

Your material or the material of your client or customer might be subject to inspection and screening for contaminants, explosives, narcotics, or any other restricted or illicit substance as it moves through the supply chain. Governments initiate these screening programs as antiterrorist and smuggling-detection programs. They mandate that packages and material be inspected to a prescribed level that will ensure that the goods are legitimate and that no other unauthorized, illicit, or dangerous material has been introduced into the legitimate supply chain. These programs often have a very specific security plan that must be applied. These are then to be integrated into your supply chain security program, as well.

Your supply chain security program should have taken into account when, where, and why the material might be subject to such scrutiny. You should also be aware of the methods used for this inspection process. For the most part, the screening process is an attempt to detect residue of the restricted material on the exterior of the package or container being processed and handled. Other types of screening employ the use of X-ray or other similar technology to gain insight into the interior of the truck or container.

Currently there are three main screening processes: ETD, X-ray, and backscatter gamma ray methodologies. ETD (explosive trace detection) is very similar to the screening process utilized on passenger baggage and carry-ons. (Refer to Section 8.6 on CCSP.) It is designed to detect the presence of chemicals that are used in the manufacture and handling of explosives. The screening process involves an application of a specialized cloth or material that would absorb the suspected chemicals. It is then examined for traces of this restricted component.

X-ray technology is an adapted methodology that will inspect the interior of parcels, packages, containers, etc. A complex algorithm screens these images of suspected prohibited materials. If you have recently traveled on a commercial airline, you and your parcels have been subject to both of these technologies. Larger versions of these detection devices are used for screening of cargo and other irregular goods and products being placed in planes, being delivered by ship, or driven in vehicle across borders.

There is another detection science that is primarily used against ocean and trucking containers: X-ray backscatter technology. It, too, develops images of the contents of a container, matched against a matrix of parameters and algorithms, but on a much larger scale. It has proved to be very useful in the detection of narcotics and human trafficking (see Figure 9.12). If your client moves material via these methods, they will be subject to these inspections. If you are responsible for the security of their material while it is handled or as it transits from region to region, you should be fully versed in this technology and be able to apply appropriate security measures to prohibit any unwarranted introduction of restricted material. Many government

Figure 9.12   Backscatter X-ray.

programs that mandate screenings can and will fine, censure, or otherwise penalize your customer or company if illegal or prohibited substances or items are found. Do not rely on them to enhance the security of your supply chain. They are looking for gaps in yours.

PART IV
CASE STUDIES

10

CASE STUDIES

10.1 Case Study 1: Ocean Container Theft, Port of Newark, NJ

A well-known manufacturer and distributor of women's intimate high-fashion clothing has been using ocean shipping to move their products from the final point of assembly into the United States for final distribution to retail outlets. The containers are full-container load (FCL), holding a variety of their products in a wide range of value, size, colors, etc. The containers are loaded, verified, and sealed at this final assembly point and trucked to the port of departure.

Since the last stage of manufacture is usually out of the same off-shore country, the ocean shipping line that handles the containers is normally the same company. The containers come into the United States at the second port of call for the ship, at the Port of Newark, New Jersey. Here they are off-loaded, clear customs, and then are trucked via the containers to several distribution houses in various regions in the United States. It is at that point where the containers are opened and the products removed. The retail value of one of these containers can range anywhere from $300,000 to nearly $1 million.

The fashion company hires the shipping line for the handling of the containers from the port of departure all the way to final destination at the regional distribution centers (DCs) in the United States. The shipping line identifies transportation providers from the U.S. port via truck to the DC.

The fashion company does not have any specific security agreement with the shipping line. Their only security concerns are that the containers be properly sealed with customs-compliant seals with verifications of the condition and number of the seal at the ports of departure and arrival and at the arrival at the DC. The fashion company is fully aware that their products are valuable both by the piece and, especially, by the shipment, but they take no other extraordinary steps of security. There is an assumption that the well-known and highly reputable shipping lines will take the appropriate measures of handling and security while the containers are in their care and custody.

On a Tuesday afternoon in late May, the ocean carrier docks at the port of Newark, New Jersey, and after off-loading and customs clearance procedures, releases the full-trailer load (FTL) of fashion products to a trucking provider for transport to a Texas distribution center. The declared value of the contents of the container is $455,000 wholesale. The actual retail value of these contents is well over $800,000.

Once the container was released, the trucking provider took the container to their holding yard, in a nearby industrial complex. It would remain there for one to three days, waiting for a truck that would take it long-haul to the Texas DC. The delay is usually caused by trying to locate a trucker who is either dropping off in the Newark area, or who can find a pickup in the Texas DC area for a turnaround to the NJ/NY area to eliminate a deadhead return.

When the truck arrives on Friday morning, a search of the yard reveals that the container is missing. More searching shows that the container was picked up on Wednesday morning by a trucker who produced a legitimate-looking pickup order. When the pickup order was provided, the yard dispatcher made a copy of it for their file and released the container. An examination of this paperwork shows it was false, that the information on the order did not truly reflect the contents of the general descriptions, that the license information of the truck was not accurate, and that the driver information was from, what turned out to be later, a stolen driver's license.

The incident was reported to both the shipping line and to the (fashion) customer. The local Port Authority of New Jersey was notified, and law enforcement opened an investigation. One of the results of the investigation was that, two days later, the empty container was found on a side street only three miles away from the trucking holding yard. To date, none of the clothing from this container has been recovered; no suspects have been developed; and no arrests have been made.

An internal security lead investigation ordered by the fashion customer was performed. While the results were not conclusive, it can be fairly agreed that the following elements of deduction are accurate. The first is that someone knew of the date and time of the delivery of the container. It could be that someone within the holding yard could have noticed the paperwork and called out to coconspirators, but the more likely scenario is the other way around—that the holding yard connection was informed it was coming, then given notice as to when it was driven to the yard. This deduction came as this yard is small, and containers are often stacked one in front of another, with early arrivals being blocked by others. This container seems to have been on the side and easily available, even though a number of other containers had arrived into that yard later on the same day.

In any event, when the trucker arrived with paperwork, a full verification was not performed. A thorough and properly followed receiving/shipping procedure would have detected inconsistencies in the paperwork.

Additional information from the investigation indicated that the destination DC had been notified by the fashion company of when to expect the container. Knowing the schedule of the ship line, one could estimate an approximate travel time (within a few days) of trucking from port to destination of when the container might show at the DC in Texas. This is not an unusual procedure, as it helps the DC to prepare for the arrival and arrange for inventory, labor, and other resources. What was interesting was that, as part of the shipping process, the ship line notified the fashion company at origin of when the container was to be off-loaded at the U.S. port. The origin office would then notify the destination DC of the expected arrival. This could also mean that this sensitive internal information could have been passed to thieves at the port to be ready for the shipment and prepare the legitimate-looking shipping documents to pick up the container at the holding yard. This would shift the focus of the investigation away from the yard operators to an internal investigation of personnel within the fashion operation itself.

In the end, nothing was proved for sure either way. However, the lesson learned by the fashion company led to changes in the shipping process and a reexamination of their supply chain security program.

10.2 Case Study 2: Pilfering within a "Knitting" and Distribution Operation

ZXC Corporation develops and markets a wide variety of technology products. Their primary business involves manufacturing and supplying goods and services to the computer industry. Another facet of their trade supplies technology for the communications industry.

Like others in their industry, they rely heavily on suppliers and providers of services for the manufacture, assembly, storage, transportation, and distribution of their goods to both B2B (business to business) and B2C (business to consumer) markets. In this particular instance, ZXC Corp. has contracted with QWE Incorporated to perform a segment of "knitting" for several of their communication products. The agreement with QWE also includes storage and distribution of the final assembled product. Transportation into the facility or out to other distributors or end users is not included in the service.

The knitting, storage, and distribution operation is located in an industrial area on the outskirts of a major metropolitan city in the Midwest. The staff and employees are a mixture of ZXC Corp. employees, QWE employees, and temporary and part-time staff supplied by a staffing agency. The staffing agency is hired by QWE Inc. as part of their labor agreement with ZXC Corp. During peak season, there is an approximate total of 115 part-time and temporary employees split fairly evenly over three shifts of a sixteen-hour workday.

The knitting portion of the operation involves the partial assembly of electronic components. The parts used in this assembly range from simple and inexpensive pieces to several small, yet rather expensive, components. Some of these small high-value pieces have adaptability features such that they can be used in other devices not isolated to ZXC Corp. products. In other words, they have value to others in the industry for other devices. The security department of ZXC is well aware of this vulnerability of these components and has a security program agreement with QWE to counteract the theft of these items.

As a regular function of the QWE operation for ZXC, cycle counts and other standard-type inventory programs are performed at regular intervals. Over the past three quarters, they have begun to notice a rise in the use from inventory of several types of these previously mentioned small high-value adaptable pieces. Once this trend was observed, the inventory process was examined for flaws or inaccuracies. None were found, and the situation was brought up as a matter of reporting and discussed at scheduled management meetings for examination, information sharing, and solution development.

QWE security is an integral member at these management meetings, typically reporting on security incidents. Hearing of the component issue, security began a reexamination of security measures that are in place for protection and antitheft of goods and components at the establishment. Security wanted to see if this was going to shake out as an inventory-management issue or, possibly, some sort of theft/pilferage from inventory. Instead of waiting for inventory engineers and risk management to complete their reviews, security felt that they could run a parallel investigation. If it should show that it could be a security breach, they are saving a lot of time and effort by not waiting days or even weeks for the others to be completed. Also, if it was a security breach—and by beginning promptly—hopefully they could identify the issue and stop the losses as soon as possible.

Considering that the components that are going missing are small and easily hidden, an examination of the search policy and procedure was conducted. The policy calls for any person coming onto, remaining on, or leaving the facility to be subject to a search of personal items, clothing, and packages or containers. If the policy was not fully understood by the guarding service responsible for the searches, or if the searches were not being performed properly and according to the published standard operating procedures (SOPs), this might account for the inability to detect the components being moved out of the building. Also examined was the CCTV system, which is strategically placed to cover the work areas of the floor as well as the inventory bins and shelves, along with other locations throughout the operation. The CCTV was checked for proper function, and then a systematic review was performed of the inventory coverage, looking for unauthorized persons or suspicious activities that could indicate pilferage. The CCTV coverage of the work areas of the operation where these components were handled was also reviewed.

Meetings with inventory managers and engineers were showing that all procedures for proper storage and handling of inventory of the pieces seemed to be in order. The conclusion of both inventory management and security was that the pieces were properly counted, logged, and tracked into and out of inventory, which moved the focus to the assembly portion of the operation. CCTV was again examined by security with the assistance of quality control. Quality control is a function that helps develop efficient assembly activities and tracks their metrics. Security thought that the quality representative might recognize errant or otherwise unusual actions or activities of the workers.

When quality was brought in to assist, security also asked about the quality function as it pertains to the activities that involve these parts: Where are they introduced into the system, and at what point is there any type of validation or other functional review for proper assembly? Quality indicated where the pieces were entered. They also indicated that the piece itself is not validated. The portion of the assembly done that involves this component is later taken to another area in the facility for other stages of knitting or assembly. It is quite possible that, if someone is stealing these pieces, it could be done at the first assembly point, during the transit to the next phase, at the second phase, or at the storage of the units that have been assembled. Before these units are released out of the building for distribution to other off-site locations, a test for function is performed. If the unit shows a malfunction, it is sent to a "repair shop" there on site. If the repair is simple, it is sent out after being fixed. If it is severe enough that it cannot be repaired, it is sent to quality for testing to determine the nature of the failure.

The result of this exercise with security and quality was a better understanding of where the missing pieces could be vulnerable. Another fact was discovered that helped explain the increase in the rotation of this valued piece. When the "repair shop" examined the units and found that this piece was missing, they simply went into inventory, retrieved the piece, and repaired the units. It was considered an easy repair that did not warrant a review by quality. Reviews of the repair shop records showed a pattern in this type of repair. It showed that when this piece was found to be missing by the shop, it was only from a very few types of units and a very few types of electronic pieces. All of the pieces involved are high value, to the tune of nearly $100, and have multiple uses for other select devices. Someone was stealing the pieces for sale to others in the industry or for those who needed these pieces for their own devices. Several dozens of these pieces were shown to be missing over the past three quarters.

Now knowing exactly where these pieces are introduced into assembly and following their movement to the phase where the repair shop might be called, another CCTV review revealed that two workers, who work closely together in a phase of assembly, seemed to be holding back on the piece and then putting the piece into their shoes. Knowing the search procedure—shoes are not examined—they knew that they could go through the process undetected.

Surveillance was set up on the suspected people, and when there was sufficient evidence to feel that they had performed the theft, they were stopped when leaving at end of their shift, and a search of the shoes discovered the stolen pieces. A corrective action plan was initiated for two updates. One was to include the random searching of shoes when the search procedure is performed. The other was for inventory management to report to quality the type and amounts of components that are pulled by the repair shop.

10.3 Case Study 3: Truck Theft

ZXC Incorporated is a U.S.-based global mobile phone technology and manufacturing company. ZXC develops and produces highly designed and engineered mobile phones for consumer use. It is also a leading developer of mobile phone software used by others in the cell phone consumer industry as well as other communications industries. They distribute throughout the world.

Their products are both high value and high risk. They are high value because a skid of phones could reach a total of $10,000 in retail value. They are high risk, as mobile phones in general are highly sought after and targeted by thieves. They are highly fluid on the black and gray markets, easily transported, and hold a relatively high value of return (points) on the thief's investment of effort and risk.

The primary manufacturing sites for ZXC are in Asia. Finished, partially assembled phones, parts, and phone peripherals are shipped to distribution points in several global regions for sale or final assembly and then transferred to distributors and other communications customers. In the United States there are two main entry points for their phones: JFK and LAX by air, and the nearby ship ports of Newark and Long Beach, if ocean shipments are used. From these entry points, they are consolidated and then moved by truck to any one of several regional distribution centers or customers throughout the country. The trucking could be by either FTL or LTL (less than full trailer load), depending upon the method of shipping (air or ocean) and the amount (volume) of product being shipped. In either case, once the products arrive in the United States, they are brought to a nearby warehousing consolidation operation, where the products are staged by subregion and loaded onto the trucks for regional deliveries. For FTLs, it is a straight long haul to destination. LTLs will have one or more stops to pick up or off-load other customer products on the way to the appointed ZXC Inc. DC.

Since ZXC products are high value and high risk, they have developed an internal supply chain security program for the protection of their goods, beginning from the place of manufacture. The supply chain security program enlists the aid and support of the security program from each of their suppliers and providers. ZXC also utilizes an audit program to measure how well their security plans are being followed. The primary focus of the security program is on secure warehouse control and handling, handoff verifications, and conditions of the products, examining for pilferage and hidden thefts.

That was the case until one Thursday in mid-October. A shipment of phones had been brought into the United States via air, arriving at JFK Airport on Tuesday. The load was examined as it was being off-loaded from the plane; all dimensions (DIMs) and counts were verified at the airport warehouse, and then the load was driven six miles to the off-site warehouse for staging and subsequent delivery. At the local warehouse, the skids of phones (finished products in this instance) were examined again for any exceptions, weight differences, and any other irregularities. The skids were staged according to the regional destinations and kept under adequate CCTV coverage.

On Thursday morning, a fifty-three-foot trailer was fully loaded with skids of ZXC Inc. phones. This FTL was destined for a distribution customer in South Florida. A long-haul trucker arrived to pick up the box, and all truck/driver information and shipping manifests/BOLs were verified. The truck left the warehouse yard at 0935 hours on Thursday. ZXC Inc. supply chain security requirements stipulated several security measures for truck transportation:

1. The load is to be sealed by an operations supervisor and the seal number documented in the shipping paperwork.
2. All truck and driver information must be verified prior to allowing the load to leave.

3. The truck is to be equipped with an active GPS system that pings a minimum of once every ten minutes.

4. The driver is to have a cell phone with contact number for both origin dispatch (JFK area) and destination warehouse operations.

5. The truck must be fully fueled at the time of loading at origin, and the driver is not allowed to stop for any reason for at least 200 miles after leaving origin. If it is necessary to stop or if the truck becomes disabled, the driver is to immediately notify both origin and destination and wait for instructions.

One of the catalysts for this additional trucking security is the fact that there are repeated thefts from trucks along major corridors in and around large metropolitan cities and trucking hubs. The point of driving at least 200 miles is to discourage thieves from following a truck or from lying in wait at local truck stops or rest areas for a truck to be left unattended. They either break into the truck container or steal the truck entirely.

When the truck arrived at the JFK area warehouse, it was operating properly and fully fueled. The driver left the facility and drove along the agreed route for 235 miles. At this point, the driver made a routine stop at a highway rest area truck stop. He called his dispatch, as directed, to notify them of this stop. He was expected to be at this stop for approximately two hours to also comply with DOT (Department of Transportation) rules on driver rest requirements.

The driver pulled into the truck parking area. There were numerous trucks and rigs in the lot there, also. He secured the truck and went to the restaurant. Since he was going to take his rest in the truck, he did not stay in the restaurant long. He later estimated he was there for only thirty-five minutes. When he returned to the parking lot, he noticed the truck and trailer missing. After a very quick check of the parking area, he called his dispatch to notify them of the stolen vehicle. Also, local law enforcement was called as well as the truck stop management and security for the property.

Many activities began to function simultaneously around this reported theft:

1. Law enforcement broadcast a full description of the truck and trailer with license plate numbers and assigned an officer to contact the driver at the rest stop.
2. The trucking dispatch notified both origin and destination of the missing truck about the event.
3. Origin contacted the customer/owner of the goods per their agreement to notify them of this theft.
4. The dispatch management opened up their GPS program for this vehicle to view current GPS information. Since the ping on the truck was set to ten minutes, it should show a fairly accurate current location.
5. The rest area security manager began to review their own CCTV system that covered the parking lot area where the driver parked the truck.

The timeline of the transport so far is

a. The truck left the distribution warehouse outside JFK at 1030 hours.
b. It was driven for 235 miles, which took approximately five hours
c. The driver secured the truck at approximately 1530 hours.
d. The truck was discovered to be missed at 1605 hours.
e. Authorities and dispatch were called within five minutes of the discovery.

Since the truck had an active GPS, which was being monitored by the trucking office, they noted that the truck had recently pinged twice at the same location. They notified the driver of the location reported by the GPS, who in turn informed law enforcement, who were already at the rest area. The location of the pings was about fifteen miles away and off the highway on a local city street. Law enforcement proceeded to this location and found the truck. However, it was only the truck that they found. It was left in a strip-mall parking area. A small window of the cab door was broken out and the ignition was punched, which allowed the truck to be started. The trailer was still missing. The trailer would only be found a week later in an off-highway parking area two states away, empty. None of the stolen phones were recovered.

There was a detailed investigation by the ZXC Inc. security management, as well as the trucking provider security officer. The end result was that all protocols and agreed procedures were followed, and they felt that the driver was not involved as a "giveaway" and cleared of any wrongdoing. Law enforcement did not identify any suspects.

A postmortem of the event by the ZXC Inc. security team, risk management, and operations managers revealed several interesting points in need of correction and updating. The first item noted was information from law enforcement. Law enforcement reported, as part of their investigation, that they routinely see organized gangs of thieves, who operate from out-of-state locations, target trucks at rest areas. These thieves go to places of distribution of desirable high-value goods and wait for the dispatch of trucks leaving the facilities. In some cases, it is suspected that inside information is passed to them to indicate that the truck has valued goods. In other situations, it is felt that the thieves take a calculated risk in selecting a truck; since it is leaving a facility full of desirable goods, then the truck must be loaded with them, too.

The thieves lay in wait for the truck and follow it until it stops for the first time. They have learned that some long hauls drive the 200-mile required distance before they stop, and the thieves are also prepared with enough fuel to make the same distance. Once the truck stops, one or two quickly break open the lock on the trailer to verify the contents, while others will break into the truck and start the cab. If they are in agreement, they take the entire rig off the highway at the very next stop, where they have another cab waiting. The trailer is transferred to this cab, and they drive to another predetermined location many miles or several states away. There they either take another trailer or several smaller trucks and off-load the contents and leave the trailer behind. The transfer point is nowhere near the end of their own "supply chain" at a storage facility or warehousing operation.

When the CCTV taken at the rest stop was reviewed, it clearly captured the activity of the thieves. It showed the truck parking, the driver locking the cab and taking a brief walk around the truck and checking the seal on the trailer doors, and then leaving for the restaurant.

Within two minutes, two people arrive at the cab of the truck on the side where the broken window was noted. In less than a minute they enter the truck and, within another minute, the truck is seen driving out of the parking area. Other views of the parking area show a small white or light-colored SUV parked near the truck, which then follows the truck out of the lot.

Using the timeline, it is estimated that they had a full thirty minutes to pull off the highway at the next exit, only six miles away, and transfer the trailer to another truck. (There was no CCTV at the strip-mall parking lot.) With six miles to drive to the next exit and another five miles to the strip mall where they transferred the trailer, the thieves had about twenty minutes to drive twenty or more miles away toward where the trailer was located two weeks later.

Another item noted was the fact that the GPS, while functioning as expected, did not follow the load. It followed the cab (truck). It was the trailer that had the value, and it was the trailer that was not equipped with any sort of GPS or location sensors.

A final point was the actual description of the vehicle. When it was reported stolen by the driver, he rightly gave a physical description of the cab and the trailer. The cab was described by color, and the driver reported that it had a company logo and other descriptors on the doors, along with the license plate number. The trailer, however, was a different story. This trailer is one typically used by long-haulers. Some companies own theirs, while many chose to lease them for operational and economical reasons. In this case, it was a leased trailer, fifty-three-foot, color white, with "barn doors." This describes about 50% of the trailers on the road today.

Working with their transportation providers with a liaison with law enforcement, as well as other technology companies who experience truck losses, ZXC Inc. security developed a corrective-action plan (CAP) to cover the gaps elucidated in the postmortem:

1. All transportation of high-value/risk goods will have dual drivers, so that while one driver is at rest, the other remains with the truck.
2. All trailers will be fitted with GPS. If the trailer does not have GPS, then there will be GPS devices embedded into the material in the truck. This will allow for tracking of the material at transfer.
3. Some identifying feature will be applied to the trailer. This was found to be difficult, since, as we indicated, the trailers are leased and owned by another company. However, in most

cases there are identifying numbering or lettering placards on the sides of the trailers to facilitate the trailer leasing account-ability. These would be noted by the driver and used for iden-tification, if needed.

There was another action item developed but not included in the CAP. It was an internal note to the business management, risk man-ager, and operations team of an important deficiency. During the investigation of whether or not all protocols were followed by the driver, it was discovered that if there was a failure by the provider's driver, the provider's liability for the loss was extremely limited. This liability only represented pennies on the dollar of the actual value of the loss. ZXC Inc. management felt that while they had insured liability on the part of a transportation provider, it did not take into account the value. That is, lesser-valued loads were on the same level as high-value ones. The end result was that the security investigation presented to the contract team that the values of transported goods varied greatly and that liability coverage should be in sync with those values. The security program showed how they varied their security requirement based on risk and value, and made suggestions to share that information with the contract and risk management teams for appropriate coverage.

10.4 Case Study 4: Parcel Network Operation Pilferage

The ASD Network Logistics Corporation operates a parcel distribution business that offers a network distribution service to companies who look to have their goods and products distributed to e-commerce end customers throughout the region. Companies that use this service are well-known e-commerce retailers offering a wide variety of consumer goods. These goods range from regular, well-known, and widely used household products to prescription pharmaceutical orders. The par-cel business is growing exponentially as the use of Internet marketing and sales have moved up next to the traditional brick and mortar retail establishments. The bulk of the products being sold and shipped to con-sumers is shipped by parcel shippers at less than first class or express handling for cost containment by both the e-retailer and the customer.

The parcel service provider intakes the goods, which have a DIM limit of less than 50 pounds, and introduces the goods into their network of regional DCs, with final delivery provided by local delivery operators. The e-retailers deliver their goods to this network provider loose. The service provider then consolidates the parcels into regions and ships them to the regional hub. The parcels are then re-sorted to subregions with address and delivery information for final delivery. The parcels are then handed off into the final stage of the network. Even though the capacity of the network has a DIM limit of 50 pounds, most of the parcels are quite small. The average parcel DIM is less than 2.5 pounds and measures approximately 2" × 6" × 12".

For transportation purposes, when the loose pieces are initially received and presorted, they are loaded into large, cardboard, open-top boxes that measure 48" × 48" × 60", known as gaylords. The gaylords are shipped to the subregions for subsorting and final delivery. During the subregional sorting, the parcels are taken from the gaylords and sorted into large plastic bins that can be easily handled by the trucking drivers and handlers.

For tracking and accounting purposes, each piece is scanned into the ASD Corporation's database using the e-commerce's own SKU (stock-keeping unit) bar code. If one of the ASD customers does not have a compatible bar-code process, ASD will apply its own bar-code tracking label. When the piece is out for final delivery to the end user, it is scanned as "delivered," and the system looks to attach the delivery information to the initial scan.

As the ASD parcel delivery network business has increased, so has the pilferage. Over the past eighteen months, management has seen an increase of "nondeliveries." This means that database reviews indicate that more and more entry scans have not been matched to delivery scan, closing the loop. In some instances, parcels were found to be mistakenly misrouted. In other instances, the delivery scans were not properly performed or were missed, or some sort of system or scan device failure contributed to nondelivery data reports.

Another potential contributing factor is that only two scans track the actual parcel. Once the parcel is initially scanned, the parcel is loaded into a gaylord. Once this occurs, the gaylord is assigned its own bar code and scanned into the system. This tracks the routing of the gaylord and associated parcels. However, there is not any matching or tracking of exactly which parcel has been loaded into which gaylord. The only thing that is tracked is the box. There is an assumption that the proper piece or parcel has been properly loaded into a gaylord destined to the same end point as the piece itself.

As the nondelivery data persists, management looks to a joint effort from both operations and security to try to determine the causes of the missing and assumed pilfered parcels, and then develop corrective action plans (CAPs) to close the gaps. The joint investigation reveals three major gaps:

1. The parcels are not unconditionally matched to the gaylord that is used to transport the piece through the network. The gaylords themselves are open to pilferage, since they are poorly covered, which allows for access to the material from the top.
2. The parcels are not unconditionally matched to the sorting bins used for the subsorting and delivery transport. The delivery bins are not securely covered, as many have missing or broken lids, which allow for access into the bins for pilferage.
3. Peripheral security systems and processes of the sorting facilities and transportation provision are poor, weak, or nonexistent.

One of the first suggestions from operations was to expand the scanning processes of the parcel as it travels through the network. This called for a piece to be scanned at least five times:

1. Upon entry from the e-retailer
2. As it is loaded into the gaylord, unconditionally matching that piece to a specific gaylord
3. Scanning the piece out of the assigned gaylord at the subsort center
4. Scanning the parcel into the subsort delivery bid
5. Scan when delivered to the end customer

Unfortunately, the present scanning system as devised does not have the capacity to hold that much data and be able to make the necessary transmissions to the database. Further, workflow measurements suggest that the time it would take to perform the multiple scans would increase handling time. In some instances, they felt they would miss some delivery deadlines, and other times constraints could be negatively affected. The use of passive RFID tags built into the SKU and/or ASD labeling was discussed. This would allow for near real-time tracking of the piece as it passed through critical portals. This was far too costly for the company to consider at this point in their developing business.

Supply chain security management partnered with operations, understanding their needs as well as their restrictions. Knowing that increased scanning and RFID were off the table, security management suggested the following:

1. Once the pieces are loaded into the gaylord, cover the gaylord with a single piece of cardboard and attach the cover to the sides of the container with security tape. The security tape would carry the logo of the company and have tamper-evident technology (TET).

2. Implement an examination procedure where the receiver of the gaylord would examine the TET tape for any signs of tampering. If any sign were evident, a manager or supervisor would be notified for further examination and possible investigation.

3. Filter out all subsort delivery bins that do not have a fitting cover. Either refit them or replace the lid and/or bin. Once the parcels are loaded into these bins, the bin will also be wrapped with company-approved TET tape.

4. Once out for delivery, the tape would be examined for tampering, prior to final delivery of the parcel.

5. Finally, facility security systems would be refitted and, where required, upgraded to be able to monitor several key operational areas, including inbound scanning, gaylord loading, subsort receiving, subsort bin loading, and TET taping.

Once the operational and security CAPs were finalized and implemented, nondeliveries were tracked for the subsequent six months and compared to the previous six-month time period. An 80% drop in nondeliveries was reported. In general terms, this appears to show that 80% more of what were previously nondelivered parcels were now making it to delivery. It is possible that the attention paid to the processes helped cause systemic improvements, but an 80% shift was significant in any event. The remaining 20% may still be attributed to the other system issues as described previously.

It is noted that this examination and CAP did not focus on internal thieves. Theft investigations could very well have identified suspects to remove them from the system. However, it would not have moved toward hardening the target and *keeping honest people honest*. Plus, the internal-theft approach setup and investigation could have taken weeks to months to complete, while other pilferages and nondeliveries would have continued at the measured rate until the suspected thieves were removed. From the perspective of limiting losses, reducing the costs of these losses, and maintaining customer service, it was decided by security and management that the best immediate business case was to close the recognized gaps as quickly as possible.

10.5 Case Study 5: Latin America Warehouse Assault

WER Computer Corporation contracted with ASD Logistics to provide both transportation and 3pls (third-party logistics supplier) warehousing and distribution services in a high-risk Latin America country. WER has used ASD several times in the past for moving their high-value and high-risk cargo into Latin America and other regions as well. There have been several instances of both pilferage and even a truck hijacking of an entire load of computers in the past in Latin America.

WER has its own security program and personnel who work with their providers in coordinating their rather strict supply chain security program. WER security also performs audits of provider facilities for compliance to their security requirements. They even go as far as to audit the transportation and handling providers used by the logistics company to determine if the logistics company is communicating and ensuring that WER supply chain security requirements are understood and implemented.

Even with having their own security program, WER relies heavily on the internal supply chain security program of ASD. They look to ASD to have their own comprehensive security program in place, no matter what any of their customers might require. WER feels that a provider who handles their valuable goods should already be responsive to the risk. It would be of concern to WER if ASD had to implement security procedures just for the WER products that would not have been in place at some level already.

As part of the agreement with WER, ASD contracted with a local warehouse provider in the Latin America country about five miles from the receiving airport. This location was chosen in coordination with the customer's delivery needs. The warehouse is in an industrial area at the perimeter of a large city with easy access to local highways. The building itself is a stand-alone structure situated in a complex of six other similar buildings. There is not any perimeter fencing or access controls, only some common entrance/exit roads.

The warehouse was outfitted with substantial CCTV coverage monitoring the access doors, overhead bay doors, and general work and storage areas. Personnel and access controls are in place, as well as an intrusion alarm for the main warehouse and the office areas.

Since this general industrial area has experienced several burglaries and other thefts, even with alarms in place, it was decided to have an armed guard service on duty when the ASD WER facility was closed in the evening. A risk analysis of the WER business at this location by the ASD security personnel discovered that response times to burglaries were slow. It was also seen that, in some past instances, a substantial amount of goods could be removed in a very short period of time, well ahead of any local law enforcement arrival. The use of an armed guard service was viewed as an additional deterrent as well as a means of providing active communication with authorities in the event of a crisis situation. The guard service would be on duty from 8 p.m. until 7 a.m. and a full twenty-four hours per day on Saturdays, Sundays, and holidays when the operation is closed.

The WER ASD operation was initiated with all security protocols and programs installed and implemented. The operation was reviewed and approved by both the WER and ASD security management.

The business had operated for approximately three months when an attempted burglary incident occurred at 0235 hours on a Thursday. The guard reported later that he was approached by a person driving a small vehicle by the front gate of the entry to the operation. This person asked if the guard had a phone to use, stating that his vehicle was broken down and that he needed to find someone to help him. As this scenario played out, at the opposite side of the complex, thieves had cut through the perimeter fencing with cutters, placing a ten-foot ladder (they brought with them) against the building to gain access to high windows. They (there were three of them) pried one window open. This open window did not trigger the alarm, since it was not covered with any contacts on the frame. Once the window was open enough, two of the thieves were able to enter the building through this window and then climb down on storage racks along the wall below the window.

The reason that there was not any alarm contacts on the window frame was because the windows of this building were ill-fitting, with gaps. Any substantial wind conditions would cause the frames to flex, which would set off normal alarm contacts. To counteract this condition, a series of motion detectors were installed on interior walls to cover the window areas. In this case, the sensors were pointed more toward the stacks of computers in the warehouse and less upon the actual windows. This allowed the thieves to make it into the building undetected. However, once they approached the material, the motion sensors activated and alarmed.

The alarms system was independent from the guard service. This means that the guard had no control over the alarm system, serving only to act as a deterrent, observer, and communicator. When the guard heard the audible alarm, he left the alleged stranded motorist and began a perimeter check. In only a moment, he happened upon three people making their way back through the hole in the fence, leaving the cutter and ladder behind. When the guard observed this, he called in to local authorities to report his findings. Once they arrived, a check of the area was performed, but no one was located, and the stranded motorist was also long gone.

A warehouse manager responded to the building, and an internal search revealed that the would-be thieves had made it to a skid of computers. It was also noticed that the bands and wrapping of this skid were cut in an attempt to access the computer cartons. Two were obviously pulled out slightly from the bulk of the others. However, none were missing. The interesting part of this piece of the investigation was that this skid of material was placed very close to the window that was accessed. Normal staging would have placed it more centrally in a marked staging area. Either this skid was overlooked and not moved into the staging area as part of the day-end shutdown process, or it was put there deliberately. This placement partially blocked the motion detector, and had it been a little closer to the window, the thieves would not even have had to climb down off the storage racks.

During the follow-up investigation, the warehouse material handler stated in his interview that the skid was overlooked from being placed in the central staging area.

ASD security would have liked to place this worker on a polygraph to try to verify the story. In this particular country, it is illegal to polygraph employees for any reason, even preemployment. In this country, only certain specific government positions have any polygraph requirements.

This is not the end of this case study. Only ten days after the burglary into the WER ASD warehouse where the alarm and guard alert prevented a potential major theft, there was another planned burglary performed. This time, the thieves learned some lessons from the first break-in. The security for the operation also learned some lessons.

Beginning with operation security, it was noted that when the guard's attention was diverted by the "stranded motorist," the activity at the other end of the property went undetected. If there was noise generated by the movement of the thieves, it was not noticed by the lone guard. The guard was alerted by the audible alarm. It was decided by ASD security, with approval from WER security, that an additional guard with a guard dog would be added to the after-hours security program. It was felt that the additional guard could cover more ground than a single guard, and adding a dog would help in detecting unusual activity and noise from other, uncovered areas of the property. This additional deterrent of a guard dog could also be used to either intimidate or track/apprehend thieves.

What the thieves learned:

1. There was a lone guard.
2. The guard was armed.
3. The guard was not connected to the alarm system.
4. The guard can be diverted.
5. The response was timed to the alarm.

It is also believed that they learned the full extent of the volume of the products contained in the warehouse. This presented an estimated value of ROI (return on investment) for the thieves.

Ten days later, at 0310 hours on a Sunday, the thieves returned. This time, they came prepared based on the lessons they had learned.

The SOP of the guards was that they would cover the property 180 degrees apart. This meant that they would patrol the perimeter, but one would always be at the opposite end from the other. In the event of an alarm or event, they would then merge at the point of the situation and contain the event as best as possible.

One of the thieves approached one of the guards near the entry/exit gate of the facility. As the suspect approached the guard that was there, the guard radioed to the other that there was someone approaching on foot. The revised SOP called for this notification procedure, and the guards were not to venture outside the perimeter of the complex for any reason.

As the suspect approached the guard, the other guard, who was also the dog handler, came over to the entry/exit area along with the other guard. Once the two guards were together and the suspect came to the gate, two other thieves appeared, both armed with handguns. The thieves threatened the guards and ordered them not to draw their guns. However, the dog handler released the dog. The dog immediately attacked the closest suspect; the guards drew their guns as one of the thieves fired on the dog, hitting it with two bullets. The guards returned fire on the three suspects. Both guards were also carrying panic alarms, which were connected to the central building alarm. One guard activated this alarm, which sounded the audible alarms and sent the standard building alarm to the monitoring station, notifying law enforcement.

As the audible alarm sounded, over a total of fourteen shots were fired back and forth between guards and suspects. No one was hit. However, the armed confrontation unnerved the would-be thieves, and they ran from the scene in different directions. The guards did not pursue, as per SOP. They phoned law enforcement and made notice of the shots fired and the injured dog. Needless to say, response by authorities was swifter than the previous burglary event from the previous week.

During the subsequent investigation that morning, it was discovered that the thieves had abandoned a stolen box truck. In the truck were bolt cutters, two floor jacks (for moving material or skids), several flashlights, and a radio scanner set to the frequency of local law enforcement. They came prepared.

A later postmortem of both burglary events considered that, during the second event, the thieves might not have anticipated the second guard and the use of a dog. They did not flee upon seeing these additional measures, but they did not seem to have enough members of their group to overpower and counteract the additional measures. Maybe they thought that the guards would submit, but the released dog, no doubt, caused the environment to change significantly enough to instigate gunfire and prompt a retreat.

One of the results of these events was that the warehouse operation was moved to a different location, where several buildings (of various businesses) were all under a controlled industrial complex, with perimeter fencing, guards, strong lighting, and perimeter patrols.

This new location did not experience any attacks for the remainder of the contract with the WER Computer Company. It was a more expensive operation, with the warehouse space being more expensive, as well as the additional security. However a joint cost/benefit analysis of operations, security, risk management, and the customer determined that a major theft could have a devastating negative impact on the operation and customers of WER.

PART V
APPENDICES

Appendix A: Sample Customer Security Requirements

**Service and Performance Contract Agreement
Between WER Industries and [The Company]**

Section 21; Security Plan Requirements

21.1 WER Industries and its affiliates make security their number one priority in their material management program. WER Industries require [The Company] team will take all necessary precautions to ensure that all WER material handled under this contract is done under the full observation of security surveillance system and personnel in the designated work areas where WER materials are handled and processed.

21.2 [The Company] also ensures that all WER material will be handled and processed in a safe and secure process that mitigates against damage, loss, or theft while in possession of WER material.

21.3 [The Company] and its subcontractors will be fully responsible for maintaining proper control and handling of the WER material in order to prevent access to the material by unauthorized individuals.

21.4 All vehicles utilized for the transportation to and from the WER facilities shall have locking and sealing capability and shall be locked and sealed with a serial numbered "bolt" seal at all times when loaded into transport vehicles.

21.5 Upon becoming aware of any intrusion, loss, or other associated security incident, [The Company] and its subcontractors will immediately report the event to WER Industries. The report will cover, but is not limited to: damage, loss, or theft of any WER material(s). [The Company's] Security Program Manager or designee will notify WER concerning the above having taken place within one (1) hour of discovery of the incident.

21.6 [The Company's] management will fully cooperate in any WER on-site security audit or survey, allowing WER security personnel the right to perform spot inspections of [The Company's] and/or their subcontractors' facility with little or no prior notification at any time during the performance of this contract.

21.7 [The Company] will maintain the following security measures for all [Company] facilities and transportation handling, storing, or transporting of WER material(s):

    21.7.1 All [Company] facilities will be equipped with intrusion alarms on all perimeter doors and windows.

    21.7.2 CCTV cameras and video recorders are inside all storage, handling, and transportation facilities.

    21.7.3 [Company] facilities will be equipped with biometric hand scanners at employee access/entrance areas.

    21.7.4 [Company] terminal facilities provide security cages for high-value goods.

    21.7.5 [Company] ID badges are required by all personnel at all locations.

    21.7.6 [The Company] will mandate that all employee use lockers at the employee entrance.

    21.7.7 All [Company] network facilities are GSUS-1 approved sites.

21.7.8   [The Company] will authorize and conduct random search policies.

21.7.9   All [Company] employees must complete extensive background checks and mandatory drug screening to include USGS-1 investigation requirements when applicable.

21.7.10 Secure chain of custody will be maintained by use of security seals on vehicles (as required).

21.7.11 Mandatory use of WER transportation security SOPs (attached) will be in place for any transportation provider contracted or used by [The Company] for the movement or transport of any WER material.

Appendix B: Sample Policy/Procedure

Transportation Provider Security

2.0 Transportation Provider(s)

Minimum security requirements for all trucking contracted by Global Mail.

Policy:

Whenever [The Company] contracts with a transportation provider to move, transport, and handle customer material of any amount, type, or value, the transportation provider must be able to provide verification that they are compliant with the [Company's] security policies and procedures for the transportation of customer material prior to being engaged in the service of transportation and handling.

2.1 Only transportation companies approved by the VP of [The Company's] Transportation will be allowed to transport any [Company] customer material.

2.2 All drivers provided by transportation vendors must be properly licensed and submit to a five (5) year criminal and motor vehicle background check.

2.3 All drivers provided by transportation vendors must first pass a drug screening.

2.4 All transportation vendors must be able to supply proof that these requirements have been met upon demand.

2.5 All transportation vendor vehicles used for terminal-to-terminal (T2T) moves must be fitted with GPS, having storage and data recovery capacity of at least thirty days.

2.6 All transportation providers will have a person assigned as their security manager who will immediately and fully investigate any and all security incidents involving [The Company's] material. This security officer will make all investigative reports and gather information associated with the security incident concerning [The Company's] material available to [Company] management upon request and allow [Company] security to work with the provider's security officer as part of the investigation.

Appendix C: Sample Security Review/Audit

FUNCTION	SECURITY MEASURE	COMPLIANT (YES/NO)	COMMENTS
ACCESS CONTROLS			
	All entry/exit doors are locked and pass keys or access cards must be used to gain entry.		
	All overhead doors are closed or secure with gates or screening when not used for loading/unloading.		
	All fire exit doors are fitted with push-bar alarms that function.		
ALARMS			
	All entry/exit doors are alarmed.		
	All overhead doors are alarmed or covered with beams or motion detectors.		
	All alarms are functional when the facility is closed for any amount of time.		
PERSONNEL ID			
	All employees are issued company ID that must be displayed on their person.		
	All visitors are verified by government photo ID and issued visitor passes.		

FUNCTION	SECURITY MEASURE	COMPLIANT (YES/NO)	COMMENTS
CCTV			
	Entire area(s) where customer material is stored and handled is covered by clear CCTV coverage.		
	CCTV coverage is digitally stored for 30–45 days.		
VEHICLE SECURITY			
	All trucks are fully locked when at bay doors.		
	All vehicles are fully locked when on deliveries.		
PROCESSES			
	All inbound scans are completed and verified.		
	All outbound scans are completed and verified.		
	All deliveries are counted and verified by receiving personnel on bills of lading (BOLs) sheets/scanners.		

Appendix D: Sample Security Budget

	YTD 2008 ACTUALS	FY 2008 BUDGET
SECURITY (COST CENTER #123-4)		
50000 Salaries & Wages		
50010 Hourly Wages		
50100 Acc. Vacation Expenses		
56030 Personnel Relocation		
56200 Car Allowance		
50310 Management Bonus		
50200 State & Fed Unemployment		
50250 Workman's Comp		
50460 Nonunion Health Benefits		
50750 Payroll Taxes		
50400 401K Company Match		
50420 Defined Benefits Pension		
54100 Telephone Expenses		
54300 Fax Lines		
54400 Web Conferencing		
54500 Cellular Phones & Pagers		
54200 Computer Lines		
52120 Motor Vehicle Rentals/Leases		
PL695320 Rent & Lease		
PL341200 Repair & Maintenance		

	YTD 2008	FY 2008
SECURITY (COST CENTER #123-4)	ACTUALS	BUDGET
56100 Car Mileage & Fuel		
56290 Toll & Parking Fees		
56295 Airlines, Trains		
56300 Hotel		
56370 Meals (Employees)		
56400 Entertainment (Customers)		
56640 Gifts		
57200 Seminars & Bus Meet		
57131 Training Meals		
58250 Noncapitalized Computer Equipment		
58260 Noncapitalized Software		
53000 Stationary, Operating Supplies		
54000 Postage Expenses		
56010 Hiring Costs & Agency Fees		
57130 Training & Subscriptions		

DIRECT OPERATING EXPENSES (DOE)

Appendix E: List of Acronyms

3pls: third-party logistics supplier
BCP: business continuity planning
BOL: bill of lading
BU(s): business unit(s)
CAP(s): corrective action plan(s)
CBP: U.S. Customs and Border Patrol
CCTV: closed-circuit television
DC: distribution center
DIM(s): dimension(s)
DOE: direct operating expense
DOT: Department of Transportation
FCL: full container load
FDA: Food and Drug Administration
FTL: full trailer (truck) load
GAAP: generally accepted accounting principles
GPS: Global Positioning System
GSM: Global System for Mobile (communications)
HVC: high-value (risk) cage
HVG: high-value (risk) goods
IT: information technology
LCL: less than (full) container load
LE: law enforcement

LTL: less than (full) trailer/truck load

OS&D: overages, shortages, and damage

POD: proof of delivery

P&L: profit and loss (statement/account)

RFID: radio-frequency identification

SKU: stock-keeping unit

SME: subject-matter expert

TET: tamper-evident technology

ULD: unit load device

VPN: virtual private network

Index